7 Numbers To Success
Roadmap for Foundries and Suppliers

Seven metrics you've never used.
And your accountant doesn't know.
That simplify oversight and give you worry-free sleep.
In less than 30 minutes a month.

The ultimate revenue defect analysis system.
GUARANTEED

Mark Mehling

Table of Contents

Introduction

The longest journey begins with a single step. Confucius

Welcome to a whole new world. Just by buying this book, you have made the first steps to building a future for your business that will outperform and outlast anything you have accomplished before.
And the journey is not that long. Or difficult.

Inside are 7 numbers that will revolutionize the way you look at the metalcasting business.

It is a *system*, not just random metrics.

It is easy to understand. In fact, many will deride its usefulness claiming it is too simple. But the best answers are usually the simplest.

You don't need a math degree, an MBA, PhD, or a crystal ball to interpret the numbers. Once you use them, the biggest question will be 'What did we do before we used these?'

There is a support network available for those who want some help implementing these numbers.

Are these numbers everything you ever need to watch in a business?
No, only the most critical to long term survival, seeing into the future, and having the confidence to sleep at night. And these are more than numbers. Each one is a string you pull that leads to answers.

This is the key to these metrics.

Most metrics are historical with little information for how to change them in the future.

These 7 are all interrelated. And each provides solutions, maps, opportunities, and answers.

For example, if Client Lifetime Value is shrinking, a concerned leadership team can evaluate Client Lifetime Value, Quote Acceptance Rate, Client Oriented Metrics, and Operational Efficiency to find the reasons.

Similarly, if profits are down but CLV remains up, Expense Creep, Operational Efficiency, and CV are the first place to look for areas to change.

All these terms are covered in detail in the book.

Is this a new system? It's a different way to look at existing operations. It uses leading indicators (talked about in the book) instead of lagging indicators traditionally used.

Why would you implement these numbers into your management?

- *Accurate forecasting based on reality instead of guessing and hoping*
- *Logical decisions and decision trees to find problems*
- *Monitor stability and/or growth. If you are satisfied with the size, output and clients you have, the numbers can monitor the stability to avoid a 2008 scenario again. If you want to grow, the P2DARE system shows the low hanging fruit.*
- *If you will be selling the foundry, these numbers will get a higher price.*

Once you see the value of this approach, there are three ways to implement it:

-on your own, using the P2DARE training and implementation package. (And this book has a free consultation with the author should you choose this method)

-on your own using an implementation advisor to help with the hurdles

-Having a 'Done-for-You' Dashboard system created that matches the needs of your facility.

No matter what you choose, the opportunities for growth in the metalcasting industry will grow worldwide over the next 20 years.

The economy will always change, competition, both foreign and domestic, will always be a challenge, and your accountant will always be a historian.

Are you ready to take control of your destiny?

Keep reading!

Mark Mehling

Don't forget to claim your BONUSES
Look at the end of this book!

Before we Begin

Who should read this book?

Owners who want to sell the business in the next 3-5 years. A sales history is one thing, but a system that predicts the future using reality based numbers, is worth a lot more to a perspective buyer.

Owners who want to avoid the '2008-2010' disaster scenario. No notice massive issues. Who don't want their accountant bleeding from the eyes with red numbers before you have a chance to take action.

CEOs/Presidents who want to sleep at night because they can keep their thumb on the pulse without being at the plant every minute.

CEOs/Presidents who want to have a simple tool to use to analyze exactly where the business stands from a future-looking perspective. And have a roadmap for fixing trouble when it appears.

CEOs/Presidents who hate long meetings where numbers are thrown around indiscriminately. Where fantasy outweighs reality in predictions.

CEOs/Presidents who want a simple set of numbers that give a chance to intervene, not just a history lesson from the past.

Marketing Managers who want to impress the boss, solve the problems others can't, and become the President, CEO, or owner of their own foundry in the near future. These numbers will blast away years of rust and corrosion, streamline thinking, and make your job *much* easier.

CFO/CPA/accountants who want to become invaluable to their employer. Instead of just slinking in with bad news, these numbers give you data the boss can actually use to make decisions about the foundry *in the future.*

Predictions

I have studied the deteriorating condition of the metalcasting industry and can make a few predictions based on that research. The number of metal casting foundries in the United States alone has dropped by nearly half between 1955 and 2000 according to the Environmental Protection Agency[1]. More than 600 foundries have closed between that report and now[2].

Can I describe you?
I am betting your foundry business employs less than 125 people. Am I right?

And 'marketing' is a confusing term that doesn't seem to be measureable.

That the CFO/CPA/accountant provides all the numbers used to measure success.

That you want a system that can predict with more accuracy than you had in 2009, when foundry profits melted and almost took down the business.

You believe *systems* for identifying problems, including sales and revenue defects, are better than gambling or RAM (Random Acts of Marketing).

The foundry has been burned by wasting money on advertising that didn't work, ad agencies who promised more than they ever delivered, and no way to measure the Return on Investment.
If any of these apply, you will love this book. Keep reading.

My Prediction
By the time you have read this book, one to three more foundries will be closer to bankruptcy. Within 10 days of reading this book, another metalcaster throw up his or her hands in frustration for having lost more quotes with no clue why.

And within 30 days, another foundry will permanently close.

Those are dramatic numbers. Without even investigating the foundries that will suffer these ignominious endings, I can also predict:

No one in their management chain has read this book.

No one in leadership embraced the concepts or implemented the strategies outlined here.

None have used the numbers revealed here to make improvements to their bottom line.

One final prediction
Every foundry owner, President and CEO that closes their doors within three years of you reading this book will blame the competition, health care, or government regulation for their closing. They will not look internally, at their own decision-making, nor at the opportunities they passed up because they believed 'my business is different'. They will throw up their hands in helpless futility, claiming they were powerless to stop the closing.

But you, on the other hand

You are different. You take control of situations. Master your own destiny. The tail doesn't wag the dog in your leadership style. You ARE the dog.

Just reading this book puts years between you and the competition.

Gives you dynamite, fuses, and even the matches to blow up past thinking.

Albert Einstein said "Insanity is doing the same thing over and over while expecting different results." You know you need some different thinking to change the results.

You know you can succeed if only you had the tools.

Welcome to the toolbox.

I am not a psychic. If, after reading this book, you implement the concepts and strategies included here, you can keep your foundry out of this cesspool of failures.

It's up to you. You can do it.

Mark Mehling

PS. Put a sticky tab on this page. Check it next year to see if my predictions are correct.

A Couple Questions...

Why is one of the books printed backwards?

The difference between the myths that must be overcome and the metrics that will propel your foundry to success are so different yet so related, I struggled with a way to show this.

I finally settled on making two distinct books but published so you had to make a real effort to change topics.

And one book is backwards from the other.

The myths will turn your backwards so that book is printed that way.

But the metrics, once applied in a system, will turn all the myths on their head. It becomes so obvious that they are myths, blasting them out of the business no longer needs dynamite- a simple pry bar will work.

So it isn't just a funny way to print a book, there is a real reason for the method.

As you read one book or the other, keep in mind that these are two sides of the same coin.

Remember:

Avoid the MYTHS

Follow the METRICS

There are two ways to success using this two-in-one book.

You have a choice.

One is not necessarily better than the other, although I do personally have a preference. Each organizational leadership team will need to evaluate the best tool for change in the environment they have.

The first way

You can go after the myths first and slay them as a gallant knight slays dragons.

And in keeping with that picture, the journey will be full of challenges. Some will argue with these points and claim they are not myths. People argued the earth was flat and the Flat Earth Society is still active. So don't be discouraged by their 'facts won't convince me' mentality.

Others will claim there is nothing that can be done- there are always dragons so live with it. This group has no interest in change, no matter how much evidence shows their lifestyle, fortune, and business are all under threat.

The status quo gives them comfort.

They don't have to learn anything new.

These are the same people who stay in their homes during floods, hurricanes, and tornadoes. Ignoring the obvious, believing it won't affect them. These are the ones who evolution describes as 'soon to be eliminated from the gene pool'. They don't care as long as there is no friction, no fence bending, no thought required.

There are also those who will defend the dragons. They not only won't help you eliminate the myths, they may actually work against the effort.

These people are actually the most dangerous.

They have such a strong belief in the myth that they will mount up in their defense. Challenge you personally, in your role as a leader, and question your abilities.

Like a lion guarding her young, they will tear at every bone and sinew they can get to keep their beliefs alive and intact.

While you are throwing a life ring, they are screaming "Swim faster! Ignore the sharks! The water is fine! There are no waves" as the poor person slips below into the blue darkness.

When you finally overcome the myths, you then implement the metrics.

Sadly, this methodology, conquering myths first, may also be like chasing butterflies- exhausting and rarely fruitful.

The second way

The second way, and the one I advocate as the most efficient, is to implement the numbers first.

You will still get those who don't believe in their usefulness, who prefer doing what they've always done. Some will take the metrics as 'gobbledygook' with no possibility of being useful. They will cite chapter and verse from some old college text to prove they were never taught the numbers. Others will question their relevance.

But implementation and repeated use of the numbers wins over the doubters. Extinguishing the breath of the fire breathing dragons. When your management team sees the results for themselves, it is easier to eliminate the myths that have tied you down the way an anchor holds a ship.

Whichever you choose, there is help available if you are confused or feel overwhelmed. The author can be reached through Debby@TheFoundryMarketer.com with your questions or to arrange a private consultation.

What are the Industry Standards for these Numbers?

When I speak at the **American Foundry Society** (AFS) and other events, someone will routinely ask this question. And it is a poor question for two reasons:

First, it's really a ruse for being able to discount their importance by comparing your business to some mythical 'industry standard'. The person asking is really looking for an outlet of reassurance that their business doesn't need to consider these numbers because their metrics are 'better than the industry average'.

Secondly, there are no industry standards! Why? Because each foundry or metalcasting supplier has such different situations that they can only be used internally. Although we haven't considered the actual numbers, yet, consider this brief intro:

The Quote Acceptance Rate is, mathematically, just the ratio of quotes accepted divided by quotes actually sent. However, if an aggressive leader implements a full-court press to get more business, they may actively stalk clients looking for opportunities. If they get 100 opportunities and 25 are accepted, their QRR is 25%. But a competitor may be only a 'quote taker', not a quote maker. Their results are 50 quotes and only 25 accepted, suggesting, incorrectly, that they have a higher QRR. That's the fallacy of an 'industry average or standard.

Look inside
Inside your own business. The phrase, impolite to some in its connotation, is true here: Mind Your Own Business. Apply these numbers regularly and you will soon be so far ahead of the industry that any numbers your competitors generate will be inconsequential to the running (and joy) of your metalcasting operation.

Clients versus Customers

What's the difference?

There is a transcendent difference between customers and clients.
I use the word '*client*' almost exclusively throughout this book on purpose.

A customer is someone who makes a purchase. That's it.

There is no real relationship established, no effort to communicate, no effort to establish trust.

The business collects no information, has no intention of communicating with the customer again.

When a customer has made their purchase, the seller now waits for another customer. Assuming someone will show up, but having no reliable method of predicting, or more importantly, *drawing* in more business.

A Client

A client, on the other hand, is someone who has trusted you enough to make a purchase.

You have started the process to bring them under your expert guidance. Like a lawyer, who has clients for an entire lifetime, you want to develop a relationship that can survive issues, problems, and challenges from other competitors.

Without being crass, it's the difference between courting and dating to build a long term relationship, and a one night stand. Although you don't actually marry buyers, there are several similarities' that can be taken from relationships:

- It takes time to build trust
- Once trust is built, it can take a few lumps here and there.
- Trust builds loyalty
- Once the relationship is established, price becomes less important.
- People are inclined to tell others of their good experience and relationship.

If I asked "Would you prefer 100 customers today, or 100 loyal clients?" which would you want? You are the one who develops and nurtures this relationship.

So I don't believe any metalcaster should have customers. That's why you will read clients throughout this book.

Leaders and managers who get this distinction will do well.

Those that do not will always struggle, sitting on the precipice of disaster. Constantly blaming the economy, cheap imports, or other moving targets.

But they are wrong. They are a product of their own making.

What is marketing?

Other than a scary word that is confusing because of its great width and depth of definition.

Most metalcasters had one or two courses, along with their engineering training, in marketing or business management. If you forgot all of it, you are on the right track.

While melting metal is pure magic, you mastered it through study and application.

It's a whole lot easier to understand marketing than it is melting metal. But it does take interest, some small amount of study, and application.

The internet

The internet has changed everything. The lines of difference between marketing, sales, and customer service are becoming blurrier all the time. The internet is just another media, but it brought choices to buyers that they previously didn't have.

Sure the huge companies, like Coca-Cola®, have massive departments full of people each claiming to be in either marketing or sales. But from your seat, trying to separate them is like trying to see the difference between fly poop and pepper!

Very simply, marketing is

Marketing is persuasion and influence. That's it. Everything else associated with the word is detail and fluff.

If you think about it, almost everything you do involves persuasion and influence. You can see how the term 'marketing', at least the old fashioned definition, is no longer valid. Consider these examples:

The real purpose of customer service is to persuade and influence customers to order again. (So they are really in marketing…)

If you could care less about getting new orders from existing clients, you don't need customer service.

Proof of this is everywhere. Just look for an organization that doesn't really worry about customers coming back. They have the worst customer service.

Examples

Consider ANY government office. They could care less if you come back so put little to no effort into CS.

How about the medical community? Most medical offices could care less if you come back. They know you will when you are sick.

And the water and electric company? You have no choice but to use their services- without competition.
And none of these mentioned do any 'marketing'.

But your business, to be profitable, had better be different.

You were in marketing years ago

We were in the persuasion and influence business (marketing) when we were 5 years old. Remember when you thought about something you really wanted? Like that horse? Or the car keys? (well, maybe not at 5...)

You thought carefully about exactly what you would say, to whom, the place and timing, and the promises you would fulfil to get what you wanted. That was all marketing. (Some people would limit that to sales, but they're narrow minded and probably have narrow wallets too...)

The whole world is marketing

Consider the decision to see a Broadway Musical. According to the dinosaurs, once you have an interest, the marketing department has done their job. When you buy the tickets, the sales department washes their hands of you. But what happens if you enter the theater, all excited, and the temperature is 95 degrees? Or you can't hear the music or actors because of the sound system? Or the dancers are wearing torn and dirty costumes?
You swear you will never go back. You tell everyone how horrible your experience was. And they tell others.

Marketing traditionalists will try to wiggle out of responsibility saying 'it was THEIR fault' and pointing to costumes, engineering, and sound production. But the real truth is that any of those faults, and hundreds of others, will stop people from coming again. You see, it's all marketing.

It's the same for you

The same is true in the foundry business. You can have the best product, great engineering, and high quality, and still go broke. Why? Because you must coordinate the People, Products, Performance and Processes to support the ultimate goal- getting more revenue by growing a herd of intensely loyal clients. Unless you are running a profit-free enterprise (and some metalcasters are...), this is your ultimate goal.

Being highly profitable is nothing to be ashamed of, either. You are taking a huge risk and should be appropriately rewarded.

Throughout this book, you may find yourself wondering how a Strategist, Management Advisor, and Marketing Consultant (me) could be talking about these numbers which don't appear to be marketing. Very simply, it's because these numbers can save a foundry through persuasion and influence.

Your engineering is already great. Your quality control is right up there. But your persuasion and influence is questionable.

But not for long… Keep reading!

"I don't need these numbers- I have an accountant…"

"There are two times in a man's life when he should not speculate: when he can't afford it and when he can." ...SAMUEL CLEMENS, ALSO KNOWN AS "MARK TWAIN" (1835-1910)

Some metalcasters will immediately dismiss the contents of this book because they have lived with more numbers than they ever wanted. And they all come from their account. And form the foundation for all decision making in the business.

Research showed none of the foundries that have closed ever used the numbers presented in these pages.

In fact, they probably all used numbers from their CPA instead.

But is your CPA/CFO really there to help you run the business?

An insolent employee?

Imagine an employee or full department that believes their work is not reviewable by you.

That follows a set of rules you didn't create and can't change.
An individual or group that you pay, but refuses any of your input into how to do their job.

You can tell them when to arrive at work, eat lunch, and go home. But other than those minor items, you have no influence you can impose.
They follow their own rules. Since you don't know the rules, you have 'trust' them.

They tell you their rules change- and you just have to trust them.

And almost none of the work they do can really be used to run the business on a daily basis.

Most CEOs would immediately fire that person. Would you?

I have just described your CFO, CPA, accountant and their department.
Did you know your CFO works for the government? But YOU pay them! How can that be?

Most CEOs or entrepreneurs believe their accountant or CFO actually works for them.

The reason is because you write his or her paycheck or pay his invoice. By paying them you believe they work for you. That there is a typical employer-employee relationship between the two of you.
Not so fast. That, unfortunately, is a myth.

Try these with your 'employee'

Before you argue your accountant is just another employee, consider these 5 points:

1. Try telling your accountant to do something with the numbers that you think might be a good idea. I guarantee you will see smoke coming from his ears. They will then explain they have a job to do, with rules already provided, and that you cannot change them.

2. Try telling your CFO or accountant how to do their job. Tell them that you want a new rule in their bean counting methodology and see how far you get.

The accounting profession, although they make some of their own rules, are under the thumb and watchful eye of the government. Every rule they institute is done to prevent government interference in their profession. To ensure the information they provide meets government standards for reporting. And will keep you, the CEO, and themselves out of jail. Try to make your own interpretations.

Any good accountant, accounting firm or CFO will fight you every step of the way. And professionally refuse, if in fact what you want falls outside generally accepted standards of the accounting profession. You may limit things that have nothing to do with accounting such is their ability to take breaks, but you cannot actually tell your CFO or your accountant how to conduct their work. But the government can…

3. Your accountant only has one real job. That job, whether you recognize it or not, is to *keep you out of jail.* (Consider this as 'wardrobe advice'- listen to him if you want to avoid an orange jumpsuit…) The whole reason you want accurate numbers for your business is to stay out of jail. Otherwise, you end up like Enron. CEOs of companies routinely go to jail because of shenanigans in their accounting departments. Some CFOs listened to their CEO and made mistakes for which they paid with jail time. Knowing their sole purpose is to keep you out of jail, a place I personally find rudely unattractive, I highly recommend allowing your accountants to do what they do best.

4. Your accountant works for the government. Or perhaps it would be more accurate to say they do the government's work. This surprises most who hear this for the first time, because, as I said previously, you are the one who signs their paycheck.

The only reason we have an entire accounting profession is so the government can collect taxes. If there were no taxes-would there really be a need for an accountant?

Other than your internal use for determining costs to ensure your profits are visible, the only reason to have an accountant is to ensure that there is a clear execution of the tax collection processes. Taxes from your business, from you, and from your employees. If none of those were ever required, there would be very little need for an accountant. You could keep the money in a bag behind your desk, dropping in revenue and pulling out expenses with no accountability. But government 'interference' changes all that.

5. Your accountant is a history major. A numerical archeologist. They tell the story of the past, not the future. They might be able to guess about the future, but it is all based on the past. And we all know that famous financial exception: "past results are not an indicator of future gains."
Same in accounting.

Theoretical history at best.

Accountants don't have the numbers you need

Your accountant cannot predict the future with the numbers that they monitor. This again is an indication that your accountant does not necessarily work for you. I would challenge you to go to your CFO or accountant and ask them to predict profits for next year, the expected sales, and the profits from current clients based on everything else determinable today.

They will gaze at you with that 'deer in the headlights' look. They are historians.

They can create mind-numbing forms and reports about last week, last month, last year, or possibly the past five years. They may tell you that they can extract the data from previous information to guess the future but that they do not have a crystal ball. That basically makes them useless in your leadership position of the company.

It's like using the years 2005-2008 to predict 2009-2012. Oops!

No insult intended

Now, I am not bashing accountants, CFO, and CPAs. As I noted, their whole purpose is to keep you out of jail. They are like lawyers- but with numbers.

Their profession was never intended to be a tool for growth and stability for the Owner, for decision making by the company President, or for the CEO to make predictive interventions for the future.

Most of these numbers are not from accounting

However, what you will find in the following pages is a series of numbers that, when assembled into a system, and reviewed regularly, accurately projects profits a year from now. Numbers with predictive qualities.
Leading indicators, not lagging results.

By assembling them into a dashboard, you get all the benefits of being at the controls of a vehicle. You see the future like the windshield, with enough information from the past like a rearview mirror. You know the health of the engine like an RPM gauge, how much gas is in the tank. And there is data like a moving GPS map to help you make turn-by-turn decisions. Pretty cool!

The numbers you will learn in this book are not taught in any school-except maybe the School of Hard Knocks. Accountants don't use them, most CEOs and entrepreneurs don't know about them, and yet they are better than gold.

These numbers have been proven in other industries. Business-to-business industries as well as B2C. You can trust these numbers. And the more you use them, the more the thought 'how did we ever live without them' will scream in your head.

By the end of this book, you will be able to use as few as 7 numbers to get an instantaneous pulse on your business. With better accuracy than a medium from Long Island- or anywhere else!

There are Only Three Ways…

Here is the simple rule of revenue: **There are only three ways to increase revenue in a for-profit business.** Only three. (And most metalcasters only use one).

> *1. Get more clients or customers*
> *2. Get your existing clients to buy more (quantity) when they buy*
> *3. Get existing clients to buy more often (increased frequency)*

To understand these three in-depth, refer to the source of revenue myth in the accompanying book.

Each of the numbers contributes to the pulse of your business with these three ways in mind.

Leading versus Lagging Indicators

For Want of a Nail

For want of a nail the shoe was lost.
For want of a shoe the horse was lost.
For want of a horse the rider was lost.
For want of a rider the message was lost.
For want of a message the battle was lost.
For want of a battle the kingdom was lost.
And all for the want of a horseshoe nail.

This classic proverb may be familiar. Its purpose is to show the importance of detail, the interconnection between small things to great occurrences, and how easy it would have been to fix the problem in the first line of the poem. It only gets more challenging as the proverb continues, to reverse the inevitable.

> *As a Naval Aviator, I was intimately involved in Aviation Safety. During an accident investigation, the primary purpose was to discover the 'lagging indicator', those pieces of the wreckage that told the story of what happened. It was too late to do anything but examine the mess that lay before me and attempt to determine the exact cause. I was essentially looking at history and attempting to determine what went wrong.*
>
> *But we examined more than just the carnage. We looked for the point at which someone could have intervened to prevent the accident. What signs, signals, or decisions were made, that, if known to all, could have prevented the accident?*
>
> *We were looking for the **leading indicators**. Those points, common to many accidents, were an accurate predictor of problems in the future.*
>
> *If we discovered the leading indicators, we could probably prevent the rest of the story.*
>
> *This is the same when looking at a foundry. Using leading indicators can reduce or eliminate the threat, while lagging indicators are the historical remains that cannot be changed.*

Imagine getting financial information about your foundry that allows intervention at the beginning of the problem ie a horseshoe nail, versus midway or later. If the General who led the battle in the poem had the data on low quantities of nails, it would have been tremendously easier to make a decision instead of losing the kingdom.

This is the concept between using leading versus lagging indicators.

Lagging indicators tell history

They are hindsight. By the time a lagging indicator tells you data, it is beyond changing. In the poem, the 'Kingdom lost' is a lagging indicator.

There is nothing to do but reflect on what happened. The lagging indicators could be researched to identify the issue to hopefully correct the problem in the future. Sadly, it can easily be too late.

Leading indicators predict

They let you intervene to reduce or eliminate a problem before it becomes a *big* issue.

Predict the future and intervene to change history.

A leading indicator gives you plausible, verifiable data to be used to make adjustments to avoid the lagging indications.

Consider most vehicles of 20 years ago. While driving back then, a flat was discovered either from the noise or someone flagging you down. That was a lagging indicator.

By the time you found out, you already had a flat. Today we have systems that warn of low pressure, giving you a yellow tire shaped light on the dash- a leading indicator which allows for action before being stuck on the side of the road.

Ignoring the leading indicator (low tire pressure light) invariably leads to having the lagging indicator (flat tire). But now that we have the leading indicator, we can intervene, avoiding the lost time, money, hassles, and danger.

Applied to Metalcasters

This is exactly the same in the metalcasting industry. Knowing the leading indicators can help avoid the lost time, money, hassles, and danger of bankruptcy. And provide a long lead time to problems, allowing for an intervention.

Unfortunately, the information provided by a CFO/CPA is just lagging indicators.

This is not a slam on their performance. The purpose of the accounting profession is not to provide crystal ball insight for running a company. Their job is specifically to keep you out of jail! Make sure you pay the right amount of taxes.

And they do a marvelous job, considering they are routinely treated with disdain for decisions that are forced on them by regulations.

Lagging indicators

What are some examples of lagging indicators in the foundry business?

Profits- When profits rise and fall, it is merely the last number computed by the accountant. By the time it's discovered profits are down, you have a huge crater to dig out of just to see sunshine. It's the famous 'bottom line'.

And as soon as you have it, it is history. What you did last month/quarter/year.

Some business owners actually squirm at their desks in anticipation, *hoping* the business made a profit!

Losses- When your CFO/CPA reports a loss, it is too late to do anything. It's history. Sure, you can patch holes by reducing costs, but that only affects the future, not the past.

Sales- By the time you discover sales are down, you already have a problem. Especially with the lead time and Q2P numbers most foundries endure.

Accounting reports- Even with the timeliness of computers, most accounting reports are available well past the time of the events. Quarterly reports, often produced 30 days later, give the leadership team almost nothing to correct that will change the past. They may be able to use the past to make changes to the future, but the history is long gone.

Lost customers- It's not easy to change foundries. Many buyers tend to stay with a known quantity than take the risk of an unknown quantity (ie new vendor.) So when a client leaves for a competitor, whether based in your country or overseas, there is usually a very good reason. (And it usually isn't price.) But once they are gone, it's like dropping your wallet overboard the boat- too late.

Like the flat tire of 20 years ago, each of these give you data too late to make corrections and decisions.

Leading Indicators

So what are some leading indicators in the metalcasting world?
Data that you can use includes Client Lifetime Value, Expense Creep, Quote Acceptance Rate, Quote Rejection Rate, and others. Each of these will trigger long before any other report can define a problem.

Client Lifetime Value

When CLV starts to dip, this is a very early indication of problems. It require more analysis but can be a customer service issue, paradigm shift of the client, economic issues, both macro and local, or other issues.

Quote Acceptance Rate

This leading indicator can show both raw numbers of quotes lost, but also dollar values of quotes lost. If the QAR is declining, in either format, there is trouble ahead. If the average lag between quote acceptance and money in the bank is 3 months, you now have a 3 month heads up of trouble. And the QAR is ripe with data for analyzing what has been accepted.

Client Valuation

Watching the growth or erosion of Client Valuations can be very instructive.

A competent leadership team recognizes that CV is a leading indicator or future stability, growth and profits. If the CV of a business is steadily rising, this is a leading indicator of efficiency, profits, lower hassles, and more loyal clients. As it falls, it is a leading indicator of trouble before it happens.

Client Oriented Metrics

For those who understand that happy clients means happy profits, Client Oriented Metrics (COM) are a leading indicator. For those who do not 'get it', they can also be a lagging indicator.

When these fall, they are a leading indicator of trouble ahead.

For metalcasters who do not worry about COM, they become lagging indicators. During an examination of why clients have gone to your competitors, non-believers will look and discover late deliveries, higher rejects rates, arguments over invoice amounts, etc.

But the clients have already lost trust. So looking now at this data, for these foundries, is only a lagging indicator. COM, used as a leading indicator, would have discovered the problems.

Operational Efficiency

Operational Efficiency, when properly tracked, is a leading indicator. As OE rises, so do profits and plant wide productivity. Once a baseline number has been established, accepting quotes with a lower OE will immediately show up on the dashboard (if you use one), well in advance of declining profits.

Quote to Paid time gap

If this is increasing, it can affect the solvency of the foundry. When clients are making fewer buy decisions in a timely manner, it may mean they are having problems, their sales are down, or they are hedging their bets. The number can also indicate buyer solvency issues that could take your hard earned money. Both cases require attention.

In summary

Leading indicators PREDICT the future.

Lagging indicators TELL the past.

Would you rather be able to tell the future or tell history stories?
Your choice.

THE NUMBERS

Client Lifetime Value (CLV)

One of the distinctions between a customer and a client (reread that section to refresh if necessary) is that you can predict revenue from clients while customers are hit or miss.

And who doesn't want to get an accurate projection of future revenue and quotes?

Client Lifetime Value is a simple, self-defining phrase. This is the amount of money, quotes if you like, that a client will generate over the number of months you can accurately predict they will remain as your client.

And it can be used in many ways, as we will see.

CLV serves many purposes. This chapter will see how it is computed for both simple and advanced achievers, and a few of the ways it can be used.

Computing CLV

CLV is actually a very simple formula. It can be further refined, but even in its simplest computation, it is meaningful.

On a single client basis:

CLV = Average Monthly Spend X Number of months as a client.

This simplified CLV can be based on historical numbers if you are just setting up a program or the most recent quotes for new clients.

Let's break that down

The number of months can be determined with a little research. Some common factors include:

- how long most clients stay with the foundry (historical average). If the average client stays with you for 33 months, use that. Averages are a good place to start and can be refined over time.
- researching the lifecycle of the casting needs. If this is a new client, and their long term need for re-orders is unclear, look for indicators in how the castings are used. Then make an estimate of how long the client will need the castings. If the initial order assumes a reorder every three months, that information can also bias your results to better accuracy.
- expectations based on previous experience of follow on orders. For current clients, order/re-order history can be used

---

Remember learning to drive?

One of the keys to stability in keeping the vehicle in the center of the lane was to look out farther ahead. If you concentrated on the road immediately in front, you ended up swaying throughout the lane.

But once you moved your eyes closer to the horizon, or much further to the future location of the car, the path became much more stable.

Client Lifetime Value works the same way. If you concentrate solely on the quote in process, you lose sight of the future, swaying from side to side financially. When you look ahead and see that a client today can potentially bring in hundreds of thousands, even millions of dollars in quotes, it changes your thinking and perception. This will stabilize the foundry's financials, too.

Average spend can also be done using historical figures to determine the

CLV of current clients, or by understanding the client's needs through your quote system.

Using CLV

Even in this simple definition, these two variables offer opportunities for both growth and stability. Influence either of these and you change the outcome. Simple mathematical principle I know, but sometimes it must be pointed out.

1. if you can increase the average spend, you increase the CLV
2. If you increase the average number of months, you increase CLV

Almost every other section of this book can be leverages to increase one or both of these variables. Grading clients and a tailored quote system can significantly increase the number of months. Understanding the source of revenue can increase the average spend. And analyzing QAR and QRR can positively influence both.

Composite CLV

CLV for the entire foundry can be determined by aggregating the data from each client into a single number. This becomes the baseline for determining acceptable variations. When CLV declines outside pre-determined levels, it's time to look at the individual clients to determine exactly the problem.

The top level CLV is an excellent reference point for ongoing monitoring. It is a tool that gives the overall health of the company, provides points to examine when there is a decrease, and gives an outlook to the future for planning.

As a leading indicator, it can be especially accurate.

CLV as a leading indicator

Once companywide CLV is determined, it can be monitored, using a dashboard, or computed regularly using a manual model.

If CLV is increasing, everyone should be happy. But don't just sit back and watch! Find out what is causing the increase and repeat it!

If CLV is decreasing, examine the variables to determine the reason. For example:

Has average spend decreased? Why? Are there customer service issues that need attention? Are the Client Oriented Metrics (see that section) falling? Is this an economic indicator? Are quantities being lowered? Why? *Are clients leaving before the predicted months?* Why? Has their need for castings changed? Why can't you fulfil their new needs? Why didn't you know they would be leaving? Did they go elsewhere for the same castings? Why?

One of the bonuses available for buying this book is a chart showing all the interrelationships between the numbers in the book. That chart alone could be worth $100K to the savvy metalcaster.

In his book *Get More Referrals Now,* author Bill Cates says *...lifetime value is not just the business a client will do with me, but the people that client will introduce me to over a lifetime.*

Better summary than I could give in a single sentence.

Why Metalcasters ignore CLV

The vast majority of foundries and suppliers keep clients for many years without paying attention to CLV. Why is this happening?

It's simply because most foundries, especially in the United States, have gotten lazy. If you find that offensive, sorry, but prove me wrong.

Foundries across the globe are a very limited capability. It takes a huge amount of capital to start a foundry. It's not a 'low barrier to entry' business, like a gasoline station.

Because of that, those who needed castings had few choices.

Until recently. But many metalcasters are living in the past where they had customers because there were so few foundries to interact with. Many foundry owners were like a big fish in a small pond.

They didn't have to do anything but answer the phone and fax. Customers sought them out. And they could treat them poorly.

But times changed. And that is why an average of 50 foundries are closing each year in the US.

What was the change?

Two primary areas: The Internet and Transportation.

The internet leveled the playing field of information. Now, if you had the capability to fill a customer's cast order, but you lived in India or China, you now had a shot at getting the order. Combined with transportation improvements, you could probably do it for cheaper.

Now customers, who had no loyalty to their current metalcaster, used the internet to find alternatives. They had no loyalty because no one at the foundry developed loyalty. (See the Loyalty Myth for a longer explanation.) And since many foundries act like commodities, customers started to buy only on price.

This is the reason for the massive migration to overseas (from the US perspective). Lower prices may have been the impetus, but lack of loyalty, being treated like clients, and having no long term relationship were also issues.

But there is still a chance

All this can be turned around by using CLV again. Once you value your customers, treating and turning them into clients, you can add stability, loyalty, and long term profitability to your existing portfolio.

Knowing, exercising, and modifying CLV is the first step.

Why implement CLV now?

The rapid rise of additive manufacturing/3D printing is a big threat to foundries. Manufacturers can now set up a small area inside their facility, or a small sub-business just outside their gates, to create products and parts and sub-assemblies that were previously only available from a foundry.

With almost no lead time, they can produce metal parts and tooling. And this technology is a sleeping giant that will only grow.

Advanced CLV

While the computation is essentially the same, consider that 'A' clients have other direct value that may not appear immediately as money. "A" clients can be expected to give referrals (cha-ching), may be induced to be part of Case Studies, are most certainly candidates for White Papers, and can be relied upon to be the backbone of the business.

Each of these factors can be added to their CLV, although not as actual cash coming to the foundry. But each of these are significant values that every client doesn't always contribute.

CLV as a budget method

Once you have mastered CLV for a client, the numbers can be used to budget for new clients. In my column 'Shaping Strategy' for **MODERN CASTING** magazine (an American Foundry Society publication), I asked the question "How much would you pay for $100?" (September 2014). Sounds like an odd question, doesn't it?

The concept, in very short terms is simple. Most metalcasters are paranoid of spending money to get clients. The struggling ones are waiting to be called, not actively seeking out the best. So very few know how to set a budget for acquiring an 'A' client.

This is where CLV can help frame the discussion.

If you know the CLV, it is like bidding for a $100 bill. If you can determine that the average client is worth $2M over their lifetime, what would you pay for that client? Like buying the $100, some only want to pay a penny. When *bidding* against others, they usually lose. Another bidder ends up buying the Ben Franklin for as little as a dollar.

If asked to pay $20,000 for a client, most metalcasters and suppliers would run in fear. Yet, comparatively speaking, that $20K for a $2M client is the same as bidding $1 for the $100 bill.

Since most foundries only look at the single order instead of CLV, they spend little or nothing. Those who know CLV will spend more- and not *that* much more- to get the best clients, with the best margins. And they can repeatedly do it with confidence knowing the numbers.

CLV gives you the perspective to budget adequately *to win!*

Remember clients?

You should have already read and understood the customer versus client discussion. CLV is a client number, while the quote amount is a customer number.

This distinction, when understood and implemented, can stabilize the business, start the path leading to higher level clients, eliminate random acts of marketing, and provide a roadmap of security. When monitored at least monthly, it also gives advance datapoints for problems with quotes, sales and revenue.

Just compute it!

Do you grade your clients?

Client Valuation (CV)

Although the liberal media would prefer to eliminate all grades from kid's schools, it's still the standard for determining progress.

It's also a fabulous way to get the most out of your client base. As much as everyone is paying their bills (hopefully), not all clients are equal. To misquote the old High School book 'Animal Farm': "All clients are equal, but some are more equal than others."

You grade every day without even thinking about it. Every buying decision on a personal level is a form of grading done to differentiate choices.

You avoid some restaurants because of the service, refuse to buy from this or that big box store. Hate shopping THERE! You are grading each of these personal suppliers.

You are graded every day, too. Your credit score is constantly used to determine your grade. Depending on that score, you get certain ads and offers. Are high end cars advertised to those with credit scores of 400? If they are, it's wasted money.

You are Graded

Your buying habits are graded and recorded. In many stores, the best buyers get different offers from the mere casual shoppers. Have you heard of the 'high rollers' who get special treatment in Las Vegas? This is just another form of grading. In this case, client grading.

Why Any Business Grades Clients

Well managed businesses are constantly grading clients to

1. Cull the best for different offers and treatment
2. Identify their characteristics so they can get more of that quality
3. Have a goal to move lower performing customers up the ladder to a higher category

It may seem awkward thinking about grading your clients. But it must be done if you want to make the most money from the time and energy invested in your business.
The 80/20 rule says 80% of your clients will be ok, while 20% will be a drain on resources. Phone calls. Complaints. Refunds. No matter what you do, it's not enough.

The same rule says 80% of all your profits only come from 20% of your customers. Don't confuse this with being the same 20% that you cannot satisfy!

The point here is that you need to grade your clients if you want to increase your income, make your best clients happier, and invest less time with problem children. And it's as simple as A, B, C.

The Ideal Client

The first step to analyze and define your BEST or PERFECT or IDEAL client. Even if you don't currently have any.

This is the perfect example, the ultimate, the client you wish everyone was.

- They buy often. And never return products.
- They understand when things go wrong. (They may not be happy, but they understand.)
- They are loyal.
- They refer you to others. They offer testimonials.
- They don't complain with every price increase.
- When the phone rings and it is them, it's a call you want to take.

Do you already have any like that?

Some objective factors

You may want to establish a more official checklist of client behaviors to truly understand your evaluations and remove some of the subjectivity. A good profile should include what you believe are optimal characteristics. These are a management decision but should include as a minimum

- Order size
- Order frequency
- Company stability
- Operational Efficiency (explained elsewhere)
- Payment terms
- Payment hassles/on time payment performance
- Order hassle factors (drawings, patterns, people, pressure, lead time, etc)
- Referrals, testimonials, Case Study prospects
- Any other critical areas you believe are important

Let the Grading Begin

Once you establish this perfect model client, all others should be measured against that profile.

Using an A, B, C, and D scale is the most simplistic way to get started with this system. Consider it this way:

An A client is one who matches most of the criteria.

Depending on your situation, you can have a steady client who doesn't order the most, but orders regularly, never complains, pays on time. Or you can have a client who buys in large quantities on an irregular basis. Or a regular buyer of large quantities who is loyal but just a little hard to satisfy. Each case is different and each application (B2B and B2C) will be different.

B clients just don't meet the A criteria.

It may be order quantity or frequency, problems, or hassles. They are not the best at payment but actually do pay within reason. They're not bad clients, but they are just not at the top level yet. With proper training and handling, they may move up to A status but aren't there yet.

C clients are there because they help pay the bills.

They will never move up to A, but have the potential to move up to B. They may have demands for your time, money or energy that can be overwhelming at times when considering the size of the order or the yearly volume. They are constantly on the phone and the staff knows who they are. They are mosquitoes- pesky but not overly dangerous, but their bite of your time leaves a mark for a while after they order. Their orders help pay the bills but you sometimes question whether they are worth the effort.

D clients

You can identify your **D clients** by asking staff, sales reps, or from your own personal experience.

These are rarely-satisfied, constantly-calling, and don't-pay-on-time people and businesses.

They challenge every penny, want everything discounted, and sap your personal strength and business energy.

Your staff physically cringes when they call. Your heart sinks when they are on the phone because you know it will be a psychologically exhausting conversation.

You don't know why you keep them as clients, but you wish they would go away.

And They Should...

They need to go away, as they are sucking up more than energy, they also eat away at your profits. They will never move up to C without a lot of effort and, even if they did, would fall back to D unless monitored more closely than you or your staff can handle.

D clients need to go-*NOW!*

Although discussing the ways to get rid of them is really beyond this book, here are two ideas:

- Raise prices until either they leave or the price makes it worth the hassle.
- Call them and have a heart to heart. Tell them you and they are not a good match. Then send them to your competitors!

An advanced concept

An advanced method of assigning grades may include the primary grade and a sub factor. For example, a B client who is always late with payment, but who retains all the other B characteristics, would be considered a B(p), or a B client for payment reasons. This advanced methodology identifies the deficient area giving you an outline for how to move them up to a full-fledged B or possibly an A. This more in-depth analysis is also useful when biasing your projections for CLV. For example, if you know that you have three B clients with payment issues, you can reduce projections accordingly.

So how does grading fit into all the other numbers?

It should be used as a coefficient when determining Client Lifetime Value. The CLV of an A client is obviously higher than a C. Lower hassles, better orders, more referrals.

Remember, the As are the ones closest to your perfect model client. So evaluating new clients within 60 days of your first order fulfillment is critical. Evaluations before that time may also be possible, but usually only the B and Cs become most visible.

When determining future sales and profits, CLV should be biased by client grading. Whether you use a formal system or formula, or simply logic and common sense, CLV becomes more accurate when you bias it with other factors besides the basic order and months retained.

CV should be used as an evaluator with Quote Acceptance Rates and Quote Rejection rates.

When you examine the reason you won or lost a lost a quote, keep track of the quality of the clients. If you find you are constantly rejected by A clients and accepted by C clients, it's time to rethink the quote process you use. There is something in your recipe that is attracting less than optimal clients.

Similarly, if you are routinely accepted by A clients, this is a validation of the process and you can relax a little more.

Does overtime go up for certain clients? Are engineering costs higher? If you have an Expense Creep (EC) issue that is traceable to a specific quote, project, or client, feed this information back into your grading.

It's not difficult

Although this may sound complicated and time consuming, it is not. Once implemented, it can be updated monthly based on feedback from your staff, reps, and your own personal experience. Unless you have hundreds of clients, the entire effort should be less than a couple hours a month. And the results should more than make up for the investment. And once a client is graded, it can be used in a dashboard and modified quarterly to influence the overall CLV, be compared against last quarter, and influence who to accept for a new client.

Another reason to grade clients

Long term relationships increase CLV as well as profits. One way to build this CLV and profit margin is through marketing that is directed to different grades of clients.

If you are not already marketing differently, sending different messages, to your A, B, and C clients (hopefully you have already dumped your Ds) it is an opportunity to build better relationships.

Would you offer the same deals to all clients equally? If so, you attract more C clients, who believe you are a bargain, than A clients, who feel slighted. Here are some simple examples of that advantage of knowing your client's grade:

-Have a complaint? Your response should be measured against their client status. You should probably do anything to make an A client happy, but spending the same effort to keep a C client is wasted money, time and energy.

-Offer different benefits to A clients than others. Perhaps different lead times, shipping options, pattern services. Then *TELL* them you are doing it based on their excellent status.

-the opposite is to impose different fees or charges on C clients. They can be used to move them up to B or to encourage them to find another source. (Yes, losing some clients can actually be more profitable.)

Client grading or Valuation can be intimidating in the beginning. However, once a system and rhythm is developed, it will lead to less hassles, higher margins, long term stability, and a better reputation.

Just do it!

Quote Acceptance Rate (QAR)

The Quote Acceptance Rate is a deceptively simple number that few research.

Of course, it can be a simple fractional assessment. If 100 quotes are sent, and 50 accepted, QAR is, in its most simplistic form, 50%. For the basic number, this is minimally acceptable for tracking progress in a long term plan.

But sophisticated metalcasters will immediately see this computation is fairly inaccurate in determining the health of the business. The advanced computation is their choice. It looks like this

Total $ Value of Accepted Quotes

Total $ Value of all Quotes Sent

This ratio more realistically asserts the actual value instead of merely raw numbers. So, if the 100 quotes sent represent $25M, total, and the accepted quotes sum to $10M of business, the *real* QAR is only 40%.

But the real value of QAR is more than just the pulse of the business.

Yes, it should be computed at least quarterly for smaller foundries, and monthly for larger plants. Understanding the growth or decline of QAR can influence decision making in areas:

WHY did we win the quote?

Any sports fans? Anyone have kids or grandkids in high school or college athletics?

Every good team watches video clips (or movies long ago) of the game and the coach analyzes the different plays with the team. Not just when they lose but especially when they win. If they don't know why they won, there is little chance of repeating it, except by luck. On the other hand, if they see certain plays that work, and repeat them, they have a much higher chance of winning again.

Do you know why you won the quote? Or are you so happy to have won, you don't ask?

Why ask?

Properly done, inquiring about why the quote was accepted builds more trust with your new or existing client.

It will also dispel the myth that price is the only reason.

But you will never know if you don't ask. And be prepared for stunned silence from the buyer initially, because very few vendors care enough to find out why the won. And fewer still why they lost.

Now what?

Once you have asked, and received a satisfactory answer, you can do several things.

Integrate that information into future quotes for *this* buyer. If the buyer chose the foundry because of past performance, leverage that information in all communications, especially quotes. For example. "We look forward to a trouble-free process again, as in the past…"

Use that information in quotes for other foundries in a similar demographic. When you analyze QAR and develop a profile (see below), you can add the 'emotional factors' you discover from asking why the foundry won. If a buyer chooses based on previous performance, and your profile identifies geography as being a dominant characteristic, emphasize the two together in future quotes. For example "Buyers choose us because of our proven past performance among all the choices available in the Western US".

Once you have several buyer's reasons, you can logically assume they apply to almost all buyers. Use that when approaching new clients, developing sales tools for your reps, and on the website front page.

Lastly, consider asking for a short testimonial once that particular quote has been filled. One or two lines from other buyers have a big influence on prospective buyers.

Characteristics of the companies & buyers

The next step is to analyze the QAR for demographic/psychographic similarities. Research and record as many details as possible about the quote and client. Include such details as:

- How large a company is your client?
- Where are they located?
- How close are they to the foundry?
- How big is the order?
- What industry is the client is?
- What industries does the casting serve?
- Is the client an OEM or a supplier?
- What shipping method do they require?
- What delivery schedule do they require?
- What type of buyer is it?
  (team/single/engineer/commodity/technical/etc)

Once all these characteristics are assembled, a clearer picture should emerge.

Compare the characteristics you discover with your defined "Perfect Client" (see section on Client Grading or Client Valuations) to understand how close you are to building a stable of great race horses.

What changes can be made to our quote system based on what was learned from the two previous questions?

If we wanted growth, where, and with who, is the foundry most successful?

The Quote Acceptance Rate (QAR) is like the story of "Acres of Diamonds" which many of you may recognize. In this great oratory, given over 5000 times, Russell Conwell, the founder of Temple University, recounts the story of the Indian man, Ali Hafed, who sold everything to search the world for diamonds. While fruitlessly expending every penny he owned, the person who bought his property discovered one of the richest diamond mines in history on the land. (The Golconda mine in India has produced such incredible treasures as the Hope Diamond.)

The 'it was right under his feet' lesson is true more often than not.

Many foundries search and struggle for new clients and new quotes, spending thousands of dollars on marketing and advertising that goes nowhere. Yet they are sitting on 'acres of diamonds' that could target the exact buyers who value them the most.

QAR is a goldmine of opportunity

You can exploit this opportunity with a little mining. Not actual mining, but data mining.

You see, every quote that you have sent has important information. You can ignore it or use it to your advantage.
Once you use the data, it changes the hunting equation entirely in your favor.

Consider a hunter that blindly goes into the woods, randomly shooting into the air for his next meal. He will expend a lot of energy, time, and bullets with few, if any, results. That's what is happening in most businesses with their marketing and client acquisition and retention systems. Lots of money and time wasted with few results.

Once you analyze QAR, compare it to the hunter who goes to property that is already stocked. And only shoots when he sees his dinner waking around. Totally different approach.

The first hunter will go hungry most of the time and be constantly frustrated. The second will not need to hunt every day unless he chooses to stock up. But he won't go hungry today because his efficient methods provided enough means to last several days.

The top ways to use QAR are simple and easy to understand.

QAR to identify trends

Back in 2009, had you been tracking QAR, you would have seen a trend developing. In either raw numbers or actual dollars, the value of what you were booking was slowing. As a leading indicator, QAR gives you both an indicator and a plan of action.

Falling QAR can be traced. Although it is easy to blame the economy, it can also be traced to a lack of planning, poor sales strategies, poor client selection and evaluation, and other factors. But no matter the reason, you know you only have two choices. Increase sales or hunker down. And QAR is a leading indicator.

QAR for building the business

Who is more likely to accept your quote? Those who are most like those who have accepted your quotes in the past. Using QAR data, identify all the attributes of those who accepted your quote in the past. These same characteristics predict who is most likely your next client. And even better, leverage this information in your quote system.

In one foundry I visited, they specialized in very small orders/ parts count. Many buyers struggle to find a foundry that can produce very small numbers of castings. Most foundries dream of getting that quote for 1,000,000 castings. This one was very happy with 10 and even less. Plus they were centrally located for ease of delivery. They had several other attributes that made them the only logical choice for many buyers. By using this data, they can assure their future by emphasizing these points, and those who use them.

By making your foundry fit the buyers' specific needs, you are much more likely to get the 'they're perfect for us!' reaction.

QAR for increasing stability

After analyzing all your clients, and understanding why they selected you, a picture emerges. Let's use a fictitious example.

Suppose the QAR analysis shows the highest acceptance rate for quotes comes from suppliers to major companies (as opposed to the OEM), within 300 miles of the plant, who order smaller quantities in a specific alloy, using green sand casting methods.

Knowing this information, quotes received that match this profile have the biggest potential to be "A" clients. The more of these type clients you receive, the better the foundry stability. If properly matched to balance more stable with cyclical industries, or boom products and recession proof casting needs, you can, over time, generate an incredibly stable platform for the future that is not susceptible to the winds of change.

QAR for identifying Client Valuations

Determine the CV profile of accepted quotes. Client Valuation (see that section) is a key indicator of loyalty, stability, and growth potential. Determining the CV of every accepted quote will also measure the quote system's performance. If 80% of all accepted quotes are C clients, there is work to be done. If 60% are A and 20% are B, it validates your methodologies for a profitably stable company.

QAR for modifying the Quote System

One of the myths from the other book is that of the 'every buyer is the same so we quote all the same'. This failure of the quote system can be overcome pretty inexpensively. And QAR data can be used.

Think of it this way. You trust other's opinions when making a decision. That is the height of social media. Well, it works the same in the buying world because all buyers are people.

If you are a buyer for a mid-level sized OEM in the Midwest, wouldn't you be more inclined to trust a foundry that is already working with mid-level OEM's in the Midwest? The point is simply this: use the data gathered from QAR to tailor the quote system to show your best side. If your quote fills more check blocks in the buyers' mind because of experience and reliability ("ABC, XYZ, and QWE all get their castings from that foundry, so they must be a good choice.."), the QAR will naturally rise.

(NOTE: If your quote system isn't really a system at all, this may mean little. The first step is to develop a system that is more than a 'this is what we charge and this is when we deliver' It is beyond the scope of this book to outline everything that should or can be included, but the first step is to find out what the industry norm is- and then do something different!)

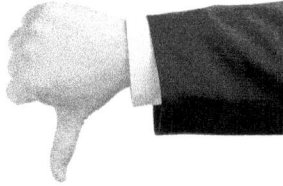

Quote Rejection Rate (QRR): The unrecognized goldmine

*If you always do what you've always done,
you'll always get what you've always got.* Henry Ford

The Quote Rejection Rate is another number that, although simple to compute, has much more use than measuring and displaying its mechanical computation.

Yes, QRR is the opposite of QAR. And it can also be measured two ways. The simplest is to count the quotes rejected and divide that by the number actually sent.

The advanced metalcaster will immediately see the advantages of the more accurate computation: Dollar Value of Quotes Rejected divided by Dollar Value of All Quotes.

So now that you have the actual number, what can you do with it?

What is a 'normal' QRR?

This common question can only be determined internally. It cannot be judged alone. QRR is influenced by other factors. And interrelated with plant capacity, operational efficiency (OE) and Client Valuation (CV).
Some metalcasters are asked for quotes all the time. Others must pursue them. Others target specific clients or orders. So there is no 'normal' in the industry.

The normal should be historically composed using data gathered before any changes are made. So look internally and determine and average number. That then becomes the baseline.

If the foundry has a 50% QRR, at 80% capacity at 75% OE (see that section), with a 'B-' average client valuation (CV), you have a much different position than a competitor with a 65% QRR at 95% capacity with an 85% OE and an 'A-' CV. While the latter QRR is 'worse' than the other, all the other stats tell a different story.

Consider this analogy

No sports team wins every time.

But they review the game, especially when they lose.

They are looking for plays that could have been called better, mistakes on their team, and process improvements to influence the next game.

How is that done today in the average foundry business? It isn't.

And that's where QRR can form a framework for analysis and change.

They wanted the quote

The basis for looking at QRR is simple. The customer sent a quote request *for a specific reason*. (Although it can be assumed they really wanted to buy castings, there may be other reasons. See appendix.) And for some reason(s) your quote was rejected.

QRR analysis needs to be analyzed against 2 distinct backgrounds: the immediate *emotional* reason and the *demographics* of the rejected quote. NOTE: Finding the immediate reason can be challenging. Sometimes using an outsider can be more productive because buyers feel less threatened by an independent third party.

Don't think emotion plays a role in the metalcasting industry? Sorry, you are wrong. As long as buyers are human, emotion will play a role. (Similar to one of my favorite bumper stickers: *"As long as there are tests, there will be prayer in schools"*).

To prove the point, just look inside yourself. There are very few people you do business with if they have, excuse my French, pissed you off. They may have the best _____ in the area (fill in the blank- restaurant, car repair, landscaping service, dry cleaning). But for some reason, they have lost your trust, confidence, and good will. Or never developed it in the first place. Or their reputation has become poor. You may make an exception and put up with them because of their skills, but most customers and clients will leave because there are plenty of choices available.

> With healthcare declining rapidly, and forecast to continue to decline due to Obamacare, finding a good doctor is getting more difficult.
> My personal physician is super! He is warm, friendly, caring, and spends more time with me than any previous doctor.
>
> But his staff is awful. Cold, impersonal, uncaring. Their phone manners stink, appointment setting skills horrible, and live behind a class enclosure in the office. (Can you imagine having a '*waiting room*' in your business?)
>
> I haven't found anyone who likes the support staff, but all love the doctor. So they remain his patient despite the staff.
>
> This is rare. Don't expect the same loyalty from clients in your metalcasting business!

First Use of QRR: Emotional Rejections

Emotional decisions can be triggered by many factors. And they are not easily separated. They routinely overlap and appear in differing amounts. The biggest factors I have discovered can be lumped in four categories:

Fear

Fear is a huge factor in any person. The fear of being fired- what will I tell my spouse and kids? Fear of being reprimanded. Fear of taking a risk and losing. All of these are eliminated by NOT taking a risk. Better to go with our previous vendor. Sure there may be problems, but at least I generally know what they are and can work around most of them. If your quote system didn't overcome these fears, it will be rejected.

You are an unknown. If the buyer has to pry out the information to alleviate their fears, they will do whatever is less work!

Trust or limiting personal risk

Why should a buyer trust you? They have been burned before with late deliveries, poor communication, and even quality problems. Foundries who close rarely deliver all their quotes before quietly closing the doors. Buyers are stranded and must scramble to find alternative sources.

What does your quote system and foundry do to build trust?

Reputation/Experience

Your reputation is out there. Through experience, website, phone skills, email- and these are just the passive indicators. When 'mad Margaret' answers the phone, buyers with questions will immediately count the attitude they hear as representing the foundry. If the website looks like everyone else's (and most do!), it reflect on the business. Unanswered email inquiries, because there is no system in place, makes buyers believe their order will receive the same treatment.

Commodity/Price Perception

President Ronald Reagan, during one of his campaigns, used the quote "If it looks like a duck and quacks like a duck..." This implied that there is only one conclusion that can be drawn. It was a duck!

So the same for commodities. If a foundry looks like it produces commodities, acts like it produces commodities, then it must be ... a commodity producer!
Commodities are chosen on price.

But there are solutions

Each of these emotional issues, once identified, can be overcome.

Fear can be overcome with education, guarantees, and warranties. Customer service and a strong quote system are also fear eliminators.

Trust is built over time but begins quickly. And is destroyed quickly, too, especially in the beginning of a relationship. Honesty, timely responses, Client Oriented Thinking®, and your quote system all help build the fortress that becomes a wall of trust, keeping competitors away from your clients.

Reputation/Experience requires education, differentiation, Client Oriented Metrics® and a website designed to solve problems (theirs not yours).

Commodity/perception emotions are solved with education, differentiation, and carefully chosen companies to sell to.

Did you think price was the number 1 reason?

You are wrong.

Because your quote system didn't answer the emotional concerns, the buyer has no other way but price to discern the difference between you and competitors. *So they chose on price.*

And this is what a buyer will use, if asked, as the reason you did not win the quote. It is the simplest, least emotional answer.

It is also logical.

But it is also false.

No buyer will pass up a value proposition that is clearly not based on price *as long as they see the value clearly!*

Metalcasters who have a high QRR have not clearly shown their value proposition versus the other quotes.

Which would YOU choose?

Consider these two quotes from a buyer's perspective:

Quote 1:
- Lead time: 6 weeks.
- Quote is per previously supplied specs by buyer.
- Price is $50K.

Quote 2:

- Lead time is normally 6 weeks however 'front of the line' priority is available for a 15% additional fee.
- We guarantee our delivery date on or before with a price reduction for every day we are late. There are no exclusions to this guarantee.
- If our castings are somehow ruined through an error in *your* process, you will receive priority 'front of the line' re-casting without an additional priority fee- pay for re-casting only.
- Our system includes weekly updates to assure you the casting process is on track.
- We guarantee our castings meet your specifications or they will be recast and reshipped at no charge on a priority basis.
- We also guarantee on-price delivery- what we quote is what you pay. No hassles, no excuses, no lawyers needed.
- Our 100% re-order rate from current clients attests to our reputation.
- Price is $52K

Any buyer who doesn't see the value in Quote 2 is a 'C' or 'D' client and you probably should let them go. Most buyers will see the huge burden lifted from their shoulders. And realize the small additional price will be repaid in lower hassles and risk. The additional cost to the foundry for quote 2 is almost zero.

The key to this hypothetical exercise is a simple rule of all human beings:

"Price is only an issue when value is unclear."

The Second QRR Use: Demographics

Once the actual reason for the rejection has been determined, it's time to look at the demographics.

It helps to define the 'rejection profile' using objective points. This exercise is not to understand the why, which was covered in the emotions section, but merely identify the characteristics of the lost quotes.

Using the profiles and demographics of location, type of business, size of business, size of quote in dollars and pieces, payment terms demanded, physical location, location relative to the plant, type buyer and similar demographics, and others, a profile is created of all quotes that were not won.

For the sake of an example, let's say this profile shows that OEMs in the Central US, in the $1B+ revenue size, asking for large parts counts, and using a commodities buyer, have a QRR of 100%.

This research serves two purposes:

1. It provides reasoning to avoid quoting if the investment is probably going to fail.

Unless 'any bid is a good bid' (poor reasoning and business sense), there is always a hesitancy to refuse to quote. However, based on the rejection profile, you can identify low return opportunities/clients and objectively decide if it is worth the investment of time, energy and money.

You are implementing a system to *objectively* determine which quotes to go after and which to decline. Think of it like hunting. Would you rather shoot at a target 100 yards away or one 10,000 yards away? And this system is like a GPS, telling you the distance!

2. This demographic profile analysis gives an 'areas to correct' mindset to determine what in this profile is causing your quotes to be rejected. A roadmap of reasons can be explored to understand their *why* which was not adequately explained by the buyer.

For instance, if you find that OEMs rarely accept your quotes, you have the beginning point for determining why.

Is there concern with you as a new vendor? Trust building and risk-reversal options abound.

Do they appear to only choose on price? A 'lifecycle price' analysis may work in your favor.

Goldmine

QRR is actually a goldmine of possible corrections. But, like any goldmine, you have to sift through everything to get to the nuggets.

Every foundry will always have rejected quotes. But while others may waste money with poorly developed marketing campaigns, or merely ignore lost quotes, your business can use this data to win better quotes from better clients.

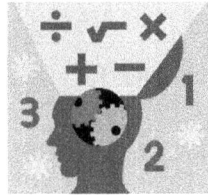

Client Oriented Metrics (COM)

As a metrically driven business society, we swoon over tables, graphs, diagrams, charts, and any other depiction of the wonderful metrics we track. Most businesses believe the metrics they track impress everyone. That's totally wrong.

Most internal metrics have no influence on buyer behavior. Why?

Very simply, buyers are human (although you might sometimes think otherwise.) Humans behave in predictable ways. And one of the dominant factors in a humans is selfishness. We all tend to look after ourselves.

Buyers are interested in themselves. What makes their job or life easier. Makes them look better to their boss. Gets them promoted. Impresses others. Gets them a raise.

Buyers are busy
Buyers are busy people. They are not devoted solely to your castings and company. You may be one of 50 different actions they must accomplish today. The car dealership example is repeated every day in the foundry world.

When you go searching for a personal vehicle, all you really want is a good price on a good car, possibly with excellent repayment terms and quick, efficient, hassle free buying experience. You could care less the age of the building, how update the service department is, or that they were the 'Dealer of the Year' chosen by the car manufacturer. Almost all these fail the "So what?" test for car buyers.

Bought a car from a dealer?

Select which of the following data or metrics swayed your decision on that particular dealer:
- *Square footage of the showroom*
- *Number of Sales people*
- *Number of cars sold last year*
- *Number of acres of used cars*
- *Number of days without an accident in the parts department*
- *Average age of the employees*

Which did you choose? If none, that's because these are not 'Client Oriented Metrics'.

If a car dealer really had it together, they would use metrics like those listed below. Which of these might persuade you to consider buying a car from that dealership?

- *Wait time for a New car delivery*
- *Time required to do paperwork*
- *Number of customers who have bought more than one car from dealership*
- *Number of times a car has to be brought back in the first 30 days*
- *Number of people who have been customers more than 10 years*
- *Number of 'we love your dealership' letters received*
- *Percentage of 'lookers' approved for credit*
- *Number of 'we loved our salesperson' letters received*
- *How many people would recommend them to friends*

See the difference?

Metalcasters could learn from this… When was the last time you looked at your website front page?? Most are all about 'me', not oriented to current and potential clients.

Nothing is different for the buyer of castings. Every buyer really just want their castings *on time, on cost, hassle free, with no hiccups*. The size of the plant, number of employees, how many acres of land they own- these also fall into the "So what?" category for the vast majority of buyers. None of these assure the on-time, on-cost, no hiccups that are critical to the buyer.

Now go and look at your website and compare it against this data. When I wrote this, a random survey of nearly 100 metalcaster's digital interface showed only one or two with useful data to a buyer.

The "So What?" test

In your personal life, this question pervades every critical look at products and services. For some, externally, while others may not even notice it occurring.

It's that doubting attitude that is born of being oversold, bombarded with marketing messages, or being conned. 50 years ago it was not nearly as prevalent as it is today. It is a defensive mechanism to reduce the chance of being ripped off. And every person employs it differently in every situation. The more cynical, or distrusting the buyer, the higher the possibility every question will be a hurdle of "So What?"

A foundry example:

"We pour 22 different alloys"

Buyer response: "So what? All I need is one."

If a point is important, it needs to be explained. This is how the "So What" test is overcome, by explaining WHY this information is important to the buyer. In the 'we pour 22 different alloys', a simple change explains why this is important:

"We pour 22 different alloys so, with our engineering and metallurgy team, we can ensure your needs for strength, flexibility, corrosion resistance, or weight requirements in your castings are met at the lowest possible cost."

What Buyers really want

In order to really understand COM, you have to understand the buyers themselves. With the various combinations of untrained generic buyers, to technical buyers, to engineers to PEs, there is not a single answer.

So how do you find out what they want, treasure, and consider minimal? Ask them!

It can be done with the simplicity of a phone call, or a standardized questionnaire using SurveyMonkey® or an equivalent.

Common denominators
However, there are some common denominators that everyone should recognize:

1. **Make my job easier**. Buyers are overwhelmed. Anything the foundry does to make the buyers' job easier will be well received.
2. **Build my trust**. Every relationship is built on trust. In the beginning, it is very low. Every buyer has horror stories of being burned because they did not double, triple, and quadruple check on a vendor.
3. **Be honest with me, even if it is a disaster**. No one likes surprises. But waiting until a minor problem becomes a catastrophe is a mistake.
4. **Be invisible from a 'needs attention' point of view**. Like the child who obediently, patiently, and quietly accompanies their parents to dinner, the movies, or even church, everyone is always shocked at the wonderful behavior. Observers are watching,

---

How many times have you heard excuses?

The list is always long. Buyers have heard them, too.

Dan Kennedy, author of many business books, relates the story of a business partner in an operation notoriously famous for employees calling in with some reason or another why they couldn't come to work. The manager got so tired of listening to the excuses, he started writing them down. At one point, he numbered each excuse. He then used this list to save time.

"Just give me the number!" became the bellow of the day.

From "No BS Ruthless Management of People and Profits" by Dan Kennedy, Entrepreneur Press, pg 17-18.

expecting the worst. When they see good behavior, it is so refreshing they tell everyone they know.

This same is true in vendor relationships. When a buyer doesn't have to check up on the order, constantly make or answer phone calls, and the castings arrive on-time and on-cost, they are shocked. It is rare that there aren't problems. And excuses.

Gathering COM

Once you really understand what is important to buyers, gathering metrics is easy. And they may form the solid foundation for bragging rights that can be used on websites, in advertising, in the quote system, and added to press releases and sales scripts.

COM will be different for each foundry, but here are a few examples to get your creative juices flowing. The COM for your specific metalcasting operation should be generated from the survey of your buyers discussed earlier in this chapter.

What is your on-time performance?

What better way to build trust than to be open about the performance a buyer can expect. Especially if yours is better than your competitors. You can even add, as part of your quote system: 'Our on-time' delivery rate of 97.5% is unmatched. Just ask our competitors!"

What is your on-cost performance?

This should also be an easy one. Publish the numbers that gives a buyer trust in your ability to deliver. And if the number is 100%, brag about that in every quote and other buyer communication!

What is the client casting reject rate?

Not the rate of rejects inside the plant, but by the end user. Buyers could care less about your internal rate, but are much more concerned with making *their* people happy. And it can also be used along the lines of 'our advanced Quality Assurance system catches defects so that we have 99% of all casting shipped are accepted by the buyers as meeting every spec for weight, quality, fit, (etc)'

How many times does a client call in to check on progress/assure their castings will show up on time?

Although rarely tracked, this is a good measure of the foundry's communication methods, how much trust has been built, and the individual buyer's attitude about the metalcaster. It's the same as your personal life. If you trust a service provider, you don't feel the need to call every hour to ensure the appointment will be kept. But when in doubt...

What methods do you use to reduce risk for the buyer?

Does the foundry use guaranteed delivery with a penalty for late? Is there a guarantee or warranty associated with the actual castings? Are they simple and easy to understand? These all eliminate risk, and buyers are very interested in lowering the risk. Properly implemented, each of these ideas will generate more much more revenue than could ever be paid out in 'adjustments'.

The mechanics are simple but different for every foundry. And they can be flexible for each quote.

Using the on-time delivery, consider this approach:

Current production and delivery time is 54 days. In the past year, 95% of all castings have been shipped within 4 days of the estimated delivery time. So propose the delivery to be 63 days, with a guarantee to the buyer of "10% price reduction for every day delivery is past (the 63rd day)."

Risk to the foundry is minimal, perceived benefit to the buyer is high.
A perfect combination.

The unfair advantage

Client Oriented Metrics are some of the most under-utilized- and essentially free- numbers used by metalcasters. They can change the internal view of every employee, too. Instead of gathering all these metrics just for internal use, the focus becomes the buyers. Too many businesses focus on the money, instead of focusing on the people or businesses that actually spend the money.

COM can help break this cycle.

I challenge you to implement this thinking. It is an untapped source of revenue and gives the foundry an unfair advantage in quotes. Use it!

Expense Creep (EC)

No, this doesn't refer to some sleazy bean counter, but to the increase in expenses either month over month or year over year. Using a *system*.

Smiling accounting staff

Finally, there is a number that your accounting department can provide! Yea! They have some use other than keeping the Feds off your door step and keeping your clothing choices to more than an orange jumpsuit. (They are valuable for that if they are doing their job properly.)

But they won't be able to help in this area unless you teach them the numbers you want. Although they have the variables, they don't routinely compute EC. And that is what you need for the dashboard quick health check view.

How to compute

EC works best as a percentage. And computing it two ways gives clarity to the information it generates. Using more volatile expense categories, each is compared as a *percentage of gross* AND *against its category* using a previous period or baseline.

An oversimplified example

Consider energy costs. How would Expense Creep (EC) be used here? Noting the two methods that are used in tandem (gross or historical), the formulas are:

First, compute as a % of gross revenue:

EC = Costs as a percent of gross revenue this month/year compared to another month/year
To be effective, there needs to be balance in the system to ensure the numbers are reflective of the period. Although monthly looks attractive, quarterly may be the best way to use this particular computation.
In this method, the number would always be positive. And it relies on an established baseline for comparison. The baseline could be from comparable historical periods or against a goal.

So if energy costs are increasing using this formula, say from a historical 6% to a new 8%, it should be noted and the second computation completed to flush out the interpretation of what has been discovered.
This is an *alert*, not an answer. It will take some research and investigation to determine the cause.

NOTE: While weekly computations can be used with several of the numbers in the system, EC can be misinterpreted if compared on a weekly basis to quotes/revenue/sales. Timing of payments, billing dates, and other variables can significantly bias weekly numbers. Use the comparison to the same category method below for weekly alerts, although even this method can lead to misinterpretation if not taken against all the data.

Secondly, compute as a % compared to historical numbers:

EC= Costs this month/year divided by Costs last month/year
(This method, by itself, is routinely used by bean counters. Alone, it can send you on a chase for no reason. Why? Because other variables can quickly affect costs.)

The calculated result, usually on either side of a value of 1, only gives a relative number. Again, it requires some investigation to understand the importance of what you just computed. If it is '1', you are looking at identical values. If the number is positive, it obviously indicates cost growth. And thus a number less than 1 suggests a reduction in expenses. No matter the result, comparison to the gross revenue will help explain the number and if, and where, further inquiry is needed.

Analyze by Combining

Combining the two perspectives can give an explanation for changes.
For example, an increase in electricity costs can be directly tied to increased production from sales orders. In this case, the creep may be visible by comparing it against last month or last year, but explained by the comparison to sales, revenue, or possibly production. A month over month EC that holds its percentage of revenue is no cause for concern.

The key to EC is the diagnosis of the aberrant figures, not the actual computation of EC alone. Without the deep dive into the reason, this number will be misinterpreted easily.

What should you measure?

There are many categories you can choose, but using simpler numbers can at least alert you to the problem of expense creep.

Using the 10 highest cost categories is a great start.

Using the top 10 most unstable numbers can be useful as long as an adequate range of values is employed.

Using 'targeted numbers' can be useful if there is a specific concern. The interrelationship of different costs can be valuable in this instance.

Sick days

The cost of sick or accident days may be an excellent way of measuring the safety awareness of the plant. If days off is spiking, find out why. It may be accidents or simply cold season. But even if it's just cold season, you may be able to slice it down with simple hand cleaners!

Shipping costs

Stories abound of shipping costs going astronomical when employees had their Christmas gifts sent to family using the company's overnight shipping account. But that would never happen in YOUR business, right?

But you may also find shipping costs increasing because low priority packages are shipped overnight just for the convenience of the person packaging. Or a price increase from a vendor that was not announced. Once researched, EC monitoring can expose vendor price changes and other hidden increases much more easily than other systems- and from a top level.

> For as long as I have been flying, there have been systems installed called 'CAUTION Panels'. These are a bank of different lights or 'annunciators', that cover all the major systems in the aircraft. They are intended to be 'leading indicators' (*see Leading and Lagging Indicators elsewhere in the book*) to alert the flight crew to possible problems ahead. Engine Oil Pressure, De-icing systems, fuel pressures, hydraulic systems- all have sensors that give a heads-up to a possible problem. With this large bank of 40+ lights amid an entire array of other information, they might not get noticed.
>
> To draw attention to the panel, a red or bright orange "MASTER CAUTION" light illuminates right in the normal field of view of both pilots. This immediately gets our attention and moves our focus to the caution panel for further investigation.
>
> Expense Creep operates this same way in a metalcaster's business, drawing attention from the myriad chores and distractions of daily operations. Expense Creep points to a possible problem by getting your attention and demanding investigation before the problem becomes larger.

How to use EC

Expense Creep acts like a light on your car dashboard that warns of a problem. Like your 'check engine' light, it doesn't tell you what is wrong, but warns of an impending failure.

EC should be the trigger that causes investigation. If the foundry establishes a range of acceptable values, EC can be especially effective by ignoring growth that is within an acceptable range of tolerance.

Used this way, when a cost/expense is out of pre-established limits, it's an opportunity to investigate and possibly correct an issue before it dramatically affects the bottom line.

For example

Energy costs may be directly related to quotes/sales, or OE. If EC is out of limits in this area, the metalcaster should have some immediate clues using OE, QAR, and costs such as scrap. Leadership may not see the increased scrap rate, but it can show up in the energy category.

Every plant/business/metalcaster/supplier is different and these correlations must be developed and applied to your specific case.

NOTE: One of the bonuses offered is the P2 DARE Quick Start Guide, which graphically portrays some of the interrelationships between the numbers. You can have it as my gift just for buying the book. See the bonuses section for the details.

Advanced Examples

Advanced analysis using EC may identify any number of challenges, from theft to larger issues. Here are a couple examples, keeping in mind every plant is different.

EC growth due to limitation of people:

Is labor cost growing without an equivalent increase in quotes or output? This could be a red flag. Why does it take more labor time for the same amount of work?

EC growth due to limitation of processes:

Older equipment can mean additional repairs and mechanical challenges. Watching this expense area creep up should alert to the need for new equipment, new processes, or different approaches to the processes.

EC growth due to limitations product:

If you see the scrap rate climb, along with labor and energy, there may have been a miscalculation about the Operational Efficiency (OE) of a quote.

EC growth due to limitations of infrastructure:

Every business reaches a limit of capacity. EC can be used is to evaluate the limitations of your infrastructure. The limit may be in one area (which becomes a bottleneck) or an overall problem.

EC growth due to procedures:

EC is so flexible, it can actually identify possible safety problems. Are sick days increasing? Work-related injuries increasing? Time off due to those injuries? Each of these may be masking a different issue that, with your intervention, can actually save a life or a disaster. By identifying and correcting an issue discovered through EC, you may be preventing a full blown catastrophe!

Limits of these examples

The scope of this book and this section is to talk about expense creep. It's not an attempt to discuss every different section of management for your business. Expense creep is a simple tool that, once put in place, raises little flags throughout your monitoring month/year. It acts as a tripwire, setting off an alarm that needs investigation.
The purpose of expense creep is to give you a tool that should be easily available for you to make decisions that will impact in the short term and in the future.

An opportunity

EC is an opportunity number. It can identify opportunities to reduce expenses through tighter control, renegotiating of agreements, or finding new sources.

While these opportunities become visible as Expense Creep, this is only a symptom, not the actual cause. But the 'red caution light' of EC can bring it to management attention for further investigation.

In summary

Do you have to wait a month or more to know that one or more expenses are getting out of line? Does your accounting staff really know how to tell if it is actually out of line?

EC is like a big CAUTION light that makes you pay attention. Before you bleed red all over the profit and loss statement. But even more than that, it lets you investigate the real reasons, make correlations that will fine tune your planning and execution, and reduce the time you lay awake at night worrying about the future.

Operational Efficiency (OE)

Operational Efficiency is a measure of how well the plant is being utilized. But not from a *machine* or *process* efficiency, from the perspective of individual quotes.

In a perfect world, every quote would use every resource of the foundry. If every quote used every process, there would be no reason to use this measurement.

Sadly, this never happens.

What actually occurs is that the business accepts quotes which only use part of its manufacturing capability. Perhaps the finishing shop is not used, or no milling or machining is required. Not every foundry has the same capabilities, so a quote will have different OE for each plant or company.

OE should be computed on an individual quote basis, and should also be compiled to be used as an overall reference number for management's use on a monthly basis.

It's subjective
Although confounding to the analytical engineering mind, OE has a significant element of subjectivity. If leadership decides to work OE very hard, a more accurate (read less subjective) system can be developed. It would assign a specific number to each capability in the plant and assign an OE based on how effectively a quote uses the aggregate number. The next paragraph suggests an alternative to eliminate subjectivity to some degree.

It's Objective

Your team should be able to easily determine which capabilities would be utilized by a particular quote. Since there are very few metalcasters with exactly the same capabilities, the internal group has the best ability to create an OE number for internal use.

For example, if only 5 different capabilities exist, using a number from 1 to 5 would be a more objective baseline.

But a highly polished system would assign a bias to each of these operations, perhaps based on margin or markup. Then a capability with a much higher markup would receive a much higher systemic number.

Now capability 2 might have a coefficient of 5, while capability 3 has a coefficient of 3. And capability 1, 4 and 5 each are assigned a 1. So a quote that uses both capability 2 AND 3 would have a higher OE than one that uses 1, 4, and 5.

Lots of numbers there so review it closely to grasp how OE can be used at both basic and advanced levels.

How is it used?

OE is an excellent addition to any quote system, including as a GO/NO-GO decision maker early on (addressed later in this section.) Each of the other items in this list can be part of the quote system, however, many metalcasters don't have a fully integrated system (or none at all), each will be called out separately.

In the Client Valuation (CV)

If you haven't reviewed the Client Valuation (CV) chapter, especially the section dealing with Best Client evaluation, now is the time.

OE is a significant bias against OE. While your Best Client should use all the capabilities of the plant, biasing those who don't is more typical. Clients who use an inordinate amount of capability need to be downgraded from the Best Client Profile.

In pricing

When accepting low OE quotes, there is substantially higher risk. These include but aren't limited to:

-risk that this order will bottleneck capability that higher value orders require.

-risk the scrap rate will balloon

-risk that fulfilling this quote will not allow accepting another quote due to time constraints

-risk that unknown costs will usurp profit

OE computed prior to pricing can be an excellent bias to preserve margin or profit.

In diagnosing EC issues

The accompanying audio talks about the relationship between OE and EC (Expense Creep).

Many metalcasters mistakenly believe that any 'any quote is a good quote'. OE can help break that myth. And comparing Expense Creep against OE can isolate the factors that are most responsible for lost profits. Generally, low OE quotes will have added impact that results in expense creep and lost profits. But you can't prove or disprove this point without analysis.

For evaluating profit and loss

When looking at revenue or profit defects, this is one area routinely overlooked. OE can provide the missing link to profitability by grading each quote. If necessary, a quick analysis based on the estimated or pre-quote OE and the actual OE evaluation at the completion of the order would be very revealing.

Measuring the relationship between OE and profit/loss may also give roads to follow for improvement.

Preventing 'Over-reach'

Sometimes, a quote is received that is not generally within the expertise of the metalcaster. Perhaps the quote is on the edge and the foundry believes it can fulfill it with just a small amount of adjustment or learning for the plant or team. However, once production starts, it becomes apparent, through the scrap rate, that the item is going to be much more challenging than expected. OE in this area could recognize this potential and be elemental in adjusting the price to ensure a fair profit is made in spite of the learning curve or scrap rate.

How to implement easily

For those just getting started with OE grading, I recommend using a simple 1-10 scale, with 10 asserting that every capability of the foundry is used. Once the system and people are comfortable using, evaluating, and systematizing this number, expand that to a 1-100 scale by taking the current 1-10 and multiplying each number by 10. Now you have the cardinal 100, 90, 80… and can start being more accurate by using refined numbers. The more accurate this computation, the more accurate all the other numbers that rely on it, such as CLV, CV, and EC.

Why isn't there an industry standard?

As pointed in other chapter, every facility has different capabilities. As such, there is no way to use any standardized OE measurements. But there are some examples that may help.

An OE of less than 10 (or 100 if you are using that scale) is normal.

The goal is to increase OE, unless it is already 100 (VERY unlikely). Many businesses have such a diversification of capabilities that only a few quotes throughout the year will ever approach 100.

However, if the internal OE for 'A' clients is 78%, this should be the comparison for all other quotes. Shooting for the 100% figure is great, however success can also be measured against the 'Best Client' profile determined from implementing the Client Valuation (CV) chapter. If your defined Best Client OE is 80%, that should be the minimum target to shoot for, and anything below that figure receive close scrutiny.

Advanced Concepts- GO/NO-GO

As was presented to the World Foundry Congress in Bilbao, Spain, OE can be computed and used as an initial GO/NO-GO number for any quote. Once implemented as a system, OE can alert leadership to quotes that could be disasters if accepted. If a 'minimum OE' figure is implemented, every quote should be analyzed for OE first to avoid wasting time now, and profits later, on those that obviously fall outside good management.

Comparison to QRR

Using the data you know about rejected quotes, comparing each one by evaluating their OE can be instructive.

Consider these questions:

-Of the rejected quotes, what was the OE of each one? Can you determine a correlation between any of the other factors that led to rejection and OE?

-Is there any correlation to OE and demographics in rejected quotes?

-Is there a correlation between OE and 'buy on price' quotes?

As each foundry considers how to communicate with buyers who initially rejected their quote, OE can save valuable time and money by eliminating those you would prefer to see not return…

Comparison to QAR

Many of these same attributes (those from QRR) and the same questions can be applied to the Quotes Accepted. This should expose other opportunities using demographics uncovered in other analyses.

After implementing this system of numbers, you should hopefully see that OE for accepted quotes is significantly higher than for rejected ones. If the situation is reversed, it bears investigation. Either the foundry has become a dumping ground, or there is not an effort to upgrade to better clients, greater profits, and long term stability.

In summary

OE is an underutilized number. While many metalcasters and suppliers are intimately familiar with the *mechanical* efficiency of their plant, few recognize how critical it is to apply this same thinking to quotes, orders, and clients.

But now **YOU** know!

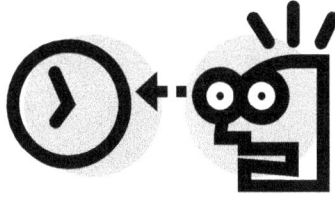

Bonus: Quote to Payment time (Q2P)

(Just for having read this far, I am throwing in a bonus number! I know, it's just another number right now, but this 'cash flow warning' can save a lot of angst.)

Perhaps one of the simplest measurements done in this system has a name that is self-defining.

Let's take the time and review a number that your accountant can track but that few ever use.

Every time you 'invest' in quoting, you have spent money. As you wait patiently to hear back from the customer or client, the clock is ticking. Bills must be paid. Lead times change. Building a backlog is necessary for stability.

This is a subset of a larger series of numbers, some of which are listed in an Appendix.

Definition

First, let's define it.

Q2P is the interval in days between the time the quote was sent and the accepted quote yielded payment.

By the definition, this only applied to accepted quotes.

The number is simple to compute. Using past records, or simply record the data as it arrives if using an online system with a dashboard, determine the date of the quote being sent to every client. Then research the date the final invoice was paid to your company.

This difference, usually in days but possibly in months or years, can be used as a bias factor in all of the numbers in this book.

Using the number

Q2P represents an investment of time and money. There is a long lead time, usually months, between the first contact of a new client with your metalcasting business, and the final money arriving in the account. This is a critical cash flow issue for smaller foundries, and certainly an additional source of money for larger ones.

This number, on a client basis, can be used to bias:

Client Valuations. Longer Q2P times are an indicator of the client's financial health, growth potential, or attitude and relationship. A 'B' customer who has an increasing Q2P should be reevaluated to see if they are slipping to a C or D. CV can have many components, tailored specifically to each foundry, but a customer who is getting slow to make decisions or pay the bills needs to be highlighted for additional scrutiny.

Client Lifetime Value (CLV). As soon as a client's Q2P starts to slip, it's time to reevaluate their CLV. There is a reason payments are taking longer to get into your bank, and Q2P acts as a tripwire to raise awareness of an impending problem. Automated systems, like a web based dashboard, can automatically build in a bias as Q2P builds, but this is also easily manually computed in smaller plants.

Other uses

Leading indicator. If the *overall* Q2P (aggregate of all clients) for the foundry is growing, this acts as a tripwire for problems ahead. A review of records from 2008/9 probably shows this number increasing as the recession started to hit. That leading indicator gives you substantially more time to start problem solving, retrenching, or making staff decisions than waiting for the CPA to rush in with red numbers.

Cash flow. The aggregate number is also an early indicator of cash flow problems. Sure, you can look at the bank balance every day and see it is shrinking, but Q2P offers a simple reason, and the methods for adjusting the long term game by biasing other numbers.

Q2P is a number with many uses. And it is simple to figure.

Now go implement it.

Summary

Will these numbers save my foundry?

If yours is a thriving foundry, on the edge, or in deep trouble, these numbers are critical.

Quote honestly, numbers alone can do nothing.

What these numbers do is immediately point out trouble spots.
But you must take action.

Every Morning…

In Robert Ringer's book "***Action- Nothing Happens Until Something Moves***", there is a lesson I found especially intriguing. I lived in Africa as a diplomat some time ago and had a chance to see how different life is there. Here is the parable Robert recounts that applies to every decision today:

"Every morning in Africa, a gazelle wakes up. It knows that it must run faster than the fastest lion or it will be killed.

Every morning in Africa, a lion wakes up. It knows that it must run faster than the slowest gazelle or it will starve.
It doesn't matter whether you're a lion or a gazelle; when the sun comes up you had better start running."

The Numbers Must be Used

The numbers in this book are the extra speed you need. They act like a personal coach to highlight weakness, train your game, and measure success using different criteria.

Just like weight sets or a treadmill. Sitting in the corner unused, they cannot improve your health. But, if used, they can be the source of untold positive change in your life.

Use these numbers, integrate them into your thinking.

Force others to think in these terms. I guarantee you will see change in your organization, your (and their) approach to problems solving, and a positive way to look trouble in the eye and laugh! Combining them into an easy-to-use dashboard will empower your every decision.

Give you tools you have never used before. Without relying on your accountant to interpret.

Make you the wisest man in your foundry Kingdom.

Because you know answers your competitors don't.

See, the foundry business is only a little about making castings. *A foundry is really a products and service business that happens to melt metal.* Sounds overly simplified? When you dig down to the bottom of the real success stories, this single attitude is pervasive throughout the organization.

You didn't miss them in school

The numbers in this book were not taught in college, so no need to wonder if you were asleep at the frat house or changing your calculator batteries when this was taught and missed them. You may have thought about them conceptually, but never understood the interrelationships. You probably just want to melt metal. And these are the numbers that allow you to spend more time doing what you love, instead of worrying about the math that keeps the doors open, pays the bills, and gives you the freedom to pursue other dreams.

But ignore these numbers at your peril. They are the same numbers that become the dead bones that are examined when a foundry goes bankrupt. They can tell the past as well as the future. You can use them, or those who look at the debris can use them.

Bottom line: Implement these numbers by changing your fundamental outlook and it will change the business.

I guarantee it.

My personal guarantee

If you use these numbers, implement them in a
dashboard, do them manually, or even keep
reports that you analyze monthly, I guarantee
you will spend less time measuring the health of
the foundry, get better sleep, and have an
incredible roadmap that you can always refer to
when it looks like a flat tire or engine trouble will slow you down.

This book, like my paid subscription newsletter, also comes with a 100X
guarantee. If you implement these numbers, I guarantee you will get more
than 100 times the cost of the book back. If not, I will offer paid for
consulting to help you find out why.

Just send me a note at Mark@TheFoundryMarketer.com to start the
conversation.

Final comments

OK, let's admit something. And it's mostly semantics.

Every business is different.

And every business is the same.

Although the *individual* challenges are different, they all fall into the same *categories*.

Your CFO/Accountant may be able to generate some of the numbers I have outlined.

But only if you tell them how you want it done. None of these are part of Generally Accepted Accounting Practices.

These are numbers to RUN your company, not to look at the past or determine how much money to pay to the thieves in Washington. If you find one or two different permutations or combinations that don't apply in your specific case- get over it.

There is more meat in these numbers than anything you learned in college.

If you can *accurately predict* the average revenue based on the numbers you derived in this short book, you will be the hero, sleep better at night, and impress everyone from your accountant to your banker.

You now have tools to do just that.

Throughout this book I've given numbers your accountant has never been able to provide and that simplify your ability to predict the future. This crystal ball ability is what you are being paid for as the CEO of a company but also is critical as an entrepreneur.

The numbers are fairly simple once you work with them a few times. You may even want to make a small crib sheet on an index card that you can keep in your desk to keep your marketing and sales people honest. (Or download the free bonus P2DARE QuickStart Guide.)

Congratulations

If these numbers have been an island in the storm for you, I would appreciate feedback at Mark@TheFoundryMarketer.com. (If all you want to do is whine and complain that your metalcasting business is different, don't waste your time, or mine, writing.)

I know some people won't get this. Reread the prediction made in the beginning of the book. Everyone at the bottom of Mt Everest who complains to the guide that it's cold will get nowhere. Chances are, if you have read this far, you are different. Congratulations.

If you want more advanced analysis and want to be able to apply this information rapidly within your business, I'm available on a limited basis as a management advisor. For information on scheduling an appointment with me please send an e-mail to Debby@TheFoundryMarketer.com to arrange an appropriate time that works for both of us.

My goal accomplished

My goal has not been to make you an expert in every field or to make assumptions and solutions in areas other than those specifically mentioned in this book.

If you think marketing is smoke and mirrors and sales is merely a question of numbers, I hope this book has opened your eyes to ways to tackle those two challenging topics. The biggest complaint of most CEOs and entrepreneurs is that marketing appears to be magic. And sometimes the Wizard (who never really explains how things operate) has confused the living snot out of you.

With these tools you now have a way to analyze what's happening. To really understand that it's not magic and not just numbers. It's a combination of using information effectively- information that you don't generally have available from the people who usually give you the numbers.

Now use them

I strongly advocate combining these numbers into a monthly reporting system. All that time spent sitting in meetings, whether with staff or the CPA, can be injected into a dashboard available in seconds at your fingertips.

You get a cardiac screening of the business in less than three minutes. Plus, with this system, you get the troubleshooting skills to fix problems.
No CPA can do that for you.

With this system of numbers, adapted specifically to your foundry, you can predict profitability using defect analysis of revenue and expense. Yes, this is the P^2/DARE system.

You have the unusual opportunity to introduce stability, profitability, and future predicting insight.

Your competitors are also reading this book. Take advantage now, before they beat you to it.

Thanks for reading.

Mark Mehling

Appendix

Other foundry metrics

I hesitated putting this chapter in here.

Too many numbers can be confusing. The 7 basic numbers used throughout this book are probably new to most readers. Adding to the confusion can really make a mess.

This section should really only be read by the most serious metalcasters.

Those who know a dashboard is the way to success, time saving, and sleeping well at night. Who want a system in place they can access from anywhere. Who know fully manual systems are only a short term fix. Who are ready to move to the advanced concepts that pay the most money. That would rather spend $100 to make $10,000 than to save a dollar to get a dollar.

This section is definitely NOT for the beginners, those who think their accountant can provide these numbers, or who believe investing in their company is just less profit. Who do not see the advantage of outsider's with vision, who want to do what everyone else does. Who 'know' the numbers won't work. Who cannot change because 'my business is different.' Just skip this section if you fall into this category.

You've been warned.

For the advanced leadership who wants to move forward, here are a few other numbers that can be used in reviews to tweak each of the other numbers to higher accuracy and therefore higher profitability.

Each of these advanced concepts/numbers/formulas are best managed through an online dashboard. For more information about these incredibly powerful tools contact Debby@TheFoundryMarketer.com specifically asking about 'P2DARE foundry *dashboards'*.

Negotiated Lost Profit -NLP

When a client makes a 'counter-quote' or an offer to do business for a price less than quoted, almost all of that difference is profit. Even if the lowered amount is because of reduced order quantity, services, etc, there is still lost profit.

Of course, many foundries pad their quote in order to be able to reduce it during the negotiations. Buyers know this and so include lower price as part of the quote analysis and acceptance procedure.

Every time the foundry accepts a quote for less than initially offered, it is profit that has been negotiated away. If 5% is normally added in as cushion, seeing a 5% NLP may be inconsequential. But if there is a 3% cushion and NLP is 5%, you need to know that.

Invoice/Quoted ratio

This ratio should always hover close to the number 1. If it starts to go negative, it indicates a real concern. Why would the invoice be less than the quote?

On the other hand, foundry methodologies must be taken into account based on individual quoting methods. For example, if the foundry quotes without shipping costs, the invoice will almost always be higher than the amount of the quote. This number relies on the knowledge of the individual quote system in your business and develops a baseline number that can be used to recognize deviations.

Quoted/Received cash ratio

Another number that should hover around 1.0, it is a leading indicator of issues inside the relationship that is costing cash.

Quote to order time interval

Another leading indicator usually influenced by factors out of your control. If this number is increasing, it indicates potential impacts from an individual client or overall impacts to the foundry. An increasing interval suggests delayed decision-making. What is slowing the decision? Hesitancy on the part of the buyer's company because they are concerned about their delivery rate, economic challenges, poor cash flow. Or many other issues. But as this creeps up, expect it to influence the top 7.

Quote to rejection time interval

Another indicator worth following. Indicates how long it takes a buyer to decide. If this is extremely short, you need to know why the quote was rejected so quickly. If the number is especially long, it's worth investigating why it took so long to eliminate.

Time from first contact to first quote

A marketing and sales timeline number that can be used as a goal. Work the system to lower the number and your profits will rise. There are many reasons why this number is large, including poor sales systems, poor contact management systems, or even something as simple as a lazy outside sales rep!

Q2P broken down to

Time between Order Completion and Final Payment (OC2FP)
This subset number shows how long you have cash flow full at risk. The order has been completed but you haven't been paid. Can also be substituted for Q2P.

Especially important if there are not progress payments which would bias Q2P.

Quote to Order time (Q2O)

This subset of Q2P can serve as a leading indicator, especially if it is increasing across all clients. Q2O is a limited measure of the decision making time required for a client to 'pull the trigger' and order.

The following two numbers indicate risk to the metalcaster the same way there are personal health indicators of risk.

Client Percentage of Gross (CPoG)

Being reliant on a small number of clients is suicide. No client should ever have more than 10% of the gross revenue without a conscious decision by leadership. Diversification ensures a balanced risk among all clients. If you rely on a single client to provide 20% of gross, the foundry must be capable of enduring a 20% revenue shortfall if that client leaves, goes bankrupt, is bought out, etc. Most businesses can take a 10% hit and bounce back, but 20%?

Client Percentage of Profit (CPoP)

This subset number of CPoG can be revealing. Used to evaluate and bias CV, it is especially useful to determine if a client is carrying their share of the profit. Much more difficult to compute than CPoG, it should be accomplished at least yearly to ensure your top clients are not using more of your capability while contributing less to profit. It will also identify low margin clients for evaluation and bias of CV and CLV.

Market Percent of Capability (MPoC)

Along with CPoG, MPoG ensures that no one market uses too much of your capability.

If 50% of production supports clients in the oil field, be ready when oil production falls off dramatically, as happened several times in my lifetime. Half of the business could be idle in a very short period. Idle means no one is buying stuff, which means no money to pay the bills.

A much smaller impact is ensuring processes and raw material diversification. Stability is also attained by ensuring no single process or alloy takes up too much of your production.

Skyrocketing costs may strangle your ability to sell. Another dark storm scenario: government regulation that imposes limits on some part of your process on which your foundry is dependent. If the process you are dependent on for steady income now requires a $600K investment to be government compliant, can you afford to shut that down AND pay the piper?

Every one of these is an advanced diagnostic intended to eliminate the fluff, speed up the arrival of money, and improve profits by efficient management of a system.

Metrics can go too far. Each of these are highly targeted. Each one causes you to lose money. They are a direct measure of lost profit or opportunity. Use them wisely or bring in an expert. For most, the admonishment 'Don't try this at home' may apply. It will only frustrate you, your team, and those who do not understand the rest of this book.

Why buyers quote competitors or multiple sources

Ever wonder why you don't win quotes? If you never ask, you probably have no idea. If you really don't research, you will fall into the 'buyers only buy on price' myth.

But every lost quote is not a foundry issue. Buyers actually have many reason to ask for a quote with no intention of every buying castings. From my experience, there are many reasons a casting buyers asks for quotes from more than one vendor. And it is rarely price alone.

The most common reasons buyers would request multiple quotes from different sources for the same product:

1. Comparison shopping. The buyer may have been buying from the same supplier for several orders and wants to ensure they are getting a fair price. They will ask other metalcasters for a quote just to keep their supplier honest, or to use your quote for negotiations with their supplier. Or the buyer may believe they are ordering a commodity. If the buyer believes the perceived value (PV) of all sources are the same, their quote request is merely comparison shopping.

2. Education. They don't know what else to ask (lack of knowledge). Depending on the buyer's experience with the casting industry, they may be asking for a quote for a department that rarely uses castings. They have no idea what to ask, who to ask, or what the difference is between all the alloys and methods. They use a quote as a source of information, hoping to learn from all the answers they receive. These can be some of the easiest quotes to win if the foundry recognizes the situation and offers some education along with the quote. An example would be a White Paper, Case Study, or even a small 'Buyer's Guide to Getting the Best Price for Castings in Ohio (fictitious title but book can be easily created at low cost.).

3. Justification. They want to confirm buying from someone else (justification). If an individual or team must justify a decision to order from foundry 'A', they may ask for a quote from 'B' and 'C' as support for their original decision. They may have had great results from their normal vendor but must re-compute every year to prove they are doing their job. By asking for several quotes, and then blowing holes in the ones they don't want to use, they confirm their choice.

4. Future Planning. Few large corporations are driven by immediate decisions. They plan well in advance. The quote request could easily be a planning tool for future purchases.

5. Second Sourcing/backup. With foundries closing on a regular basis, buyers are afraid they may place an order that is never filled. So a back-up plan is needed and the rejected quote may be held to the side as insurance should the primary winner fail to perform or deliver. Or the company may actually place a small order to try the foundry out.

6. Research. The buyer is not happy with nor excited to do business with their primary metalcaster. So begins the search for an alternative. Asking for a quote is one method of getting information.

So each of the quotes you offered has some purpose. Deciphering the reasons the quote was rejected is an invaluable tool. This is one reason QRR can be so productive. Once you know the reason you quote was rejected, it should stimulate an entirely different approach to continued contact with the buyer.

Bonuses

Bonus #1
A **FULL YEAR** of the M4 Short Sheet

"Mark's Monthly Musings for Metalcasters", known as the M4 Short Sheet, is sent via email 12 times a year ($120 value). Full of easy to implement NOW items. Easy-to-read, directly to the point, and a full page crammed with actionable ideas.

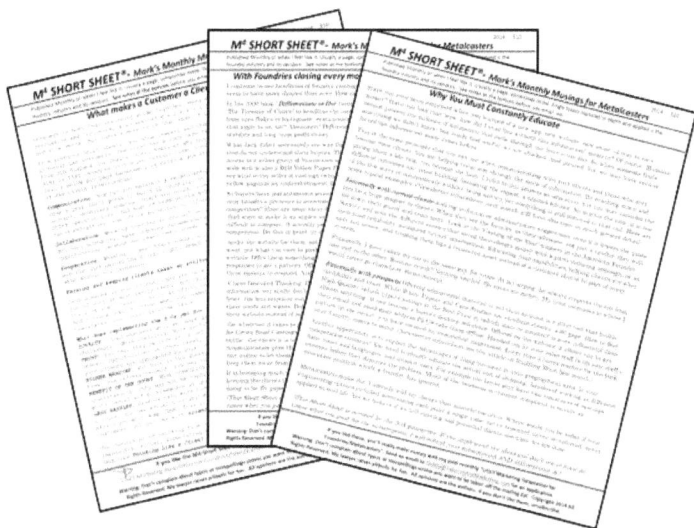

To claim this bonus, send an email to
debby@TheFoundryMarketer.com
with "M4 SHORT SHEET" in the subject line.
You will be added to the list for a FULL YEAR!

Bonus #2

P²DARE* QuickStart Interrelationship Diagram

Understanding the inter-relationship between each of the numbers, how they interact with each other, influence one another- it can be complicated until you get used to using the them.

As a bonus for buying this book, you can receive a copy of the P²DARE QuickStart Guide Chart, a $99 value, completely free.

Keep it handy when reviewing the numbers after the system is set up. Or use it as a cheat sheet to analyze how a change in one area affects others.

To receive your copy, email *debby@TheFoundryMarketer.com* with "FREE CHART" in the subject line and a pdf copy will be sent right back!

The **P²/DARE** Foundry System
Perfect Profits by Defect Analysis of Revenue and Expenses

QuickStart Guide
Interrelationship Diagram

METRIC	COMPUTATION	REVEALS	LEVERAGE	CORRELATIONS
CLIENT LIFETIME VALUE- CLV	Average monthly spend X Months as a client	Predicts Revenue, Sales, Profit	Influence other variable to increase CLV and CLV-p	All other metrics
CLIENT LIFETIME PROFIT- CLVp	(CLV - ECL) blended with CV, CLP and OE	Predicts profit/loss with high accuracy		
CLIENT VALUATIONS OR CLIENT GRADING - CV	Individual to each foundry and client	Quality of clients based on your specific foundry		
OPERATION/ EFFICIENT	Specific		Early Warning S!	EC, OE, /

*Profit prediction through defect analysis of revenue and expenses

BONUS #3

Free 20 minute consultation
($150 value)
When you order the
P2/DARE*
Do-it-Yourself Course
for only $297 +s/h

The P^{2}DARE system gets you on-track fast. Have your own system up and running quickly with this 5 CD/workbook success kit. But you may still have questions. Use this bonus to get a 'barrier breaking' 20 minute consultation with Mark Mehling. Ask anything. Unique problem? Don't understand a point? Need a resource?

Redeemable Certificate included with P^{2}DARE system

To schedule your personal consultation, email
Debby@TheFoundryMarketer.com

*Profit Prediction by Defect Analysis of Revenue and Expenses

BONUS #4
Real newsletter, NOT email!

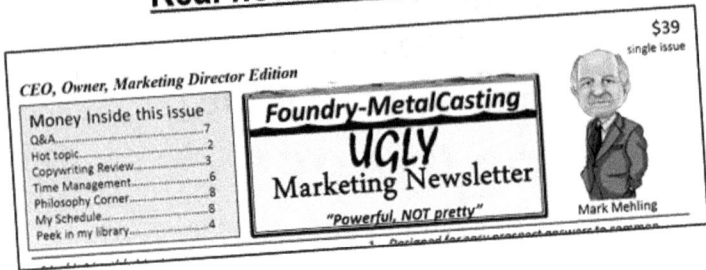

$39
single issue

CEO, Owner, Marketing Director Edition

Money Inside this issue
Q&A.....................7
Hot topic...............2
Copywriting Review.....3
Time Management........6
Philosophy Corner......8
My Schedule............8
Peek in my library.....4

Foundry-MetalCasting
UGLY
Marketing Newsletter
"Powerful, NOT pretty"

Mark Mehling

Three Full Issues of my Monthly
UGLY Marketing Newsletter
for Metalcasters/Vendors
Just pay $5/mo ($10 overseas) printing-mailing cost

There are pretty newsletters, full of colorful pictures of Santa and bunnies. Then there is the UGLY Marketing Newsletter, with just basic Black and White, but crammed full of actionable ideas.

Every month you can fill your brain with simple, easy-to-implement ideas to increase sales, increase the Quote Acceptance Rate, modify websites and sales materials to increase effectiveness, analyze poor examples, refine existing systems and consider new approaches.

You get 3 months of this paid newsletter subscription FREE! Then continue at a discounted rate or cancel anytime. Each issue has the 20X guarantee- if you implement the ideas and don't see 20X the cost of the newsletter within a year, I will refund that issue and still continue the newsletter for 6 months FREE!

Send an email to debby@TheFoundryMarketer.com for a full application. Offer valid only with Credit Card.

END
7 Numbers To Success:
Roadmap for Foundries and Suppliers

END
7 Myths That Shackle Foundry Profit$

BONUS #4
Real newsletter, NOT email!

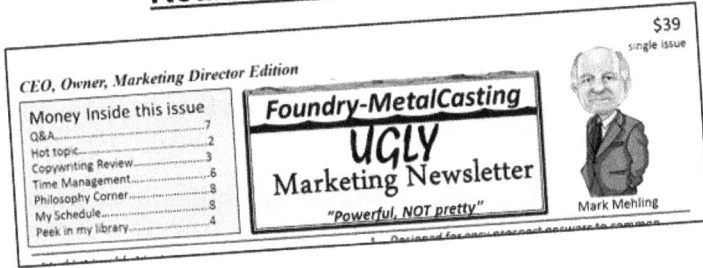

CEO, Owner, Marketing Director Edition

Money Inside this issue
Q&A.................................7
Hot topic..........................2
Copywriting Review............3
Time Management..............6
Philosophy Corner.............8
My Schedule......................8
Peek in my library..............4

Foundry-MetalCasting
UGLY
Marketing Newsletter
"Powerful, NOT pretty"

$39
single issue

Mark Mehling

Three Full Issues of my Monthly
UGLY Marketing Newsletter
for Metalcasters/Vendors
Just pay $5/mo ($10 overseas) printing-mailing cost

There are pretty newsletters, full of colorful pictures of Santa and bunnies. Then there is the UGLY Marketing Newsletter, with just basic Black and White, but crammed full of actionable ideas.

Every month you can fill your brain with simple, easy-to-implement ideas to increase sales, increase the Quote Acceptance Rate, modify websites and sales materials to increase effectiveness, analyze poor examples, refine existing systems and consider new approaches.

You get 3 months of this paid newsletter subscription FREE! Then continue at a discounted rate or cancel anytime. Each issue has the 20X guarantee- if you implement the ideas and don't see 20X the cost of the newsletter within a year, I will refund that issue and still continue the newsletter for 6 months FREE!

Send an email to debby@TheFoundryMarketer.com for a full application. Offer valid only with Credit Card.

BONUS #3

Free 20 minute consultation
($150 value)
When you order the

P2/DARE*

Do-it-Yourself Course
for only $297 +s/h

The P^{2}DARE system gets you on-track fast. Have your own system up and running quickly with this 5 CD/workbook success kit. But you may still have questions. Use this bonus to get a 'barrier breaking' 20 minute consultation with Mark Mehling. Ask anything. Unique problem? Don't understand a point? Need a resource?

Redeemable Certificate included with P^{2}DARE system

To schedule your personal consultation, email
Debby@TheFoundryMarketer.com

*Profit Prediction by Defect Analysis of Revenue and Expenses

Bonus #2

P²DARE* QuickStart Interrelationship Diagram

Understanding the inter-relationship between each of the numbers, how they interact with each other, influence one another- it can be complicated until you get used to using the them.

As a bonus for buying this book, you can receive a copy of the P²DARE QuickStart Guide Chart, a $99 value, completely free.

Keep it handy when reviewing the numbers after the system is set up. Or use it as a cheat sheet to analyze how a change in one area affects others.

To receive your copy, email *debby@TheFoundryMarketer.com* with "FREE CHART" in the subject line and a pdf copy will be sent right back!

*Profit prediction through defect analysis of revenue and expenses

Bonus #1
A *FULL YEAR* of the M4 Short Sheet

"Mark's Monthly Musings for Metalcasters",
known as the M4 Short Sheet, is sent via email 12 times
a year ($120 value). Full of easy to implement NOW
items. Easy-to-read, directly to the point, and a full page
crammed with actionable ideas.

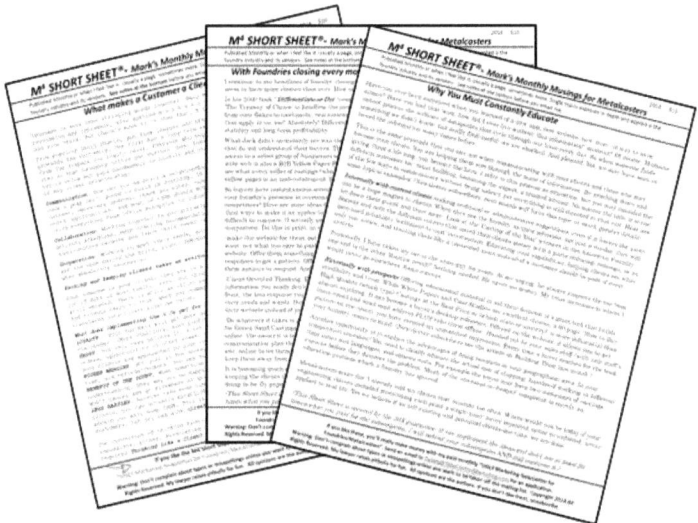

To claim this bonus, send an email to
debby@TheFoundryMarketer.com
with "M4 SHORT SHEET" in the subject line.
You will be added to the list for a FULL YEAR!

Congratulations!

You have finished reading the 7 biggest myths that can close any business, but especially metalcasters and their suppliers.

As a reminder, these myths were:

- *"My Business is Different" Myth*
- *The Loyalty Myth*
- *The High Quality Myth*
- *The Source of Revenue Myth*
- *The Source of Profit Myth*
- *Buyers Only Buy on Price Myth*
- *The Quote System Myth*

Review the bonuses on the following pages. They are my gift for purchasing the book.

If you have not read the 7 numbers that can eliminate these myths, turn the book over and start reading.

Recognizing the problem is the first step toward the cure.

You have completed the first step to ensuring your business is stable, attracts clients like a magnet, and is profitable. Now read how to measure your newfound success.

Do it now!

Mark Mehling

challenged, or sent to competitors. And there would be no relationship, no credit for past work, on time deliveries, or other factors.

But we know that is not true. Just like the decisions we make in our personal lives, industrial buyer's value many more factors than price alone.

[1]US Title 48 FAR 9.103(c) (emphasis mine).

Buyers Only Buy on Price Myth Addendum

But What If?

Of course, there is always the challenge offered "What if the buyer is paid a bonus for lowest price? How do you overcome that?"

First, I personally would want proof that this arrangement is common.

> The largest industrial buyer in the world, the US government, doesn't buy non-commodities solely on price (in spite of what you may have heard).
>
> "The award of a contract to a supplier **based on lowest evaluated price alone can be false economy**... While it is important that Government purchases be made at the lowest price, this does not require an award to a supplier solely because that supplier submits the lowest offer."[1]
>
> If the government has figured out that buying the lowest bid is not smart (shocking!), certainly a for-profit industry has done the same...

Look around at all the 'cheapest' options that are available. Paying lowest price, ignoring value, would get a buyer fired! The reliability of the Mercedes in the example from the front of the book compared to the Yugo would immediately mandate the purchase of the higher priced item. The value is actually a lower lifetime cost to the owner.

Secondly, if lowest price is actually the primary driver with all casting buyers, why would a client stay with a foundry for years? Many metalcasters keep clients for 5-10 years without so much as a complaint. If price were truly the ONLY point of decision, every quote would be

What's that look like?

A completely generic, grossly over simplified sample is this:

As they say in commercials: your mileage may vary. Use this *concept*, not this exact example…

Transparency trumps politics

Predetermined cost cuts are much less political when implemented this way, thus avoiding strife when they must be imposed. In the heat of a disaster or downturn, it removes a lot of emotion.
It's easy to see the data, so there are not a lot of surprises.

Decisions made in the cool clear-headedness of an office will trump the slash and burn tendencies of fighting for survival when trouble hits.

One Solution

The following system is based on three specific foundational principles:
  1. Adequate costs controls are already in place.
  2. This system has been reviewed by those affected BEFORE it is implemented.
  3. Cuts are not made in areas that can increase revenue, quotes, sales, etc. This includes client service and areas that would reduce *Client Oriented Metrics* (see that section).

The system itself is accomplished through a simple chart.

Across the top is the percentage reduction in quotes/sales/revenue, such as 5, 10, 15, 20, 30, and 50, 75, and 100%. (You could also consider planning cost cuts in the event of a natural disaster, however keep in mind each of these will be reflected in the revenue reductions ie a natural disaster may reduce production and revenue by 75%, therefore use that column.)

Down the side, use separate lines for the 15 highest expense categories. This may include overtime, travel, energy, labor etc. Each of these could also be broken down as a subset once you master the first iteration.

In the main body of the table, a decision is made at each intersection.

		REVENUE DROP			
		10%	20%	30%	50% ....
EXPENSES					
LABOR					
	OFFICE	no change	?	?	OUTSOURCE 50%
	MANAGEMENT	no change	?	?	
	PLANT FLOOR	no change	?	Single Shift only	
	SUPERVISORS	no change	?	?	
	SHIPPING	no change	50% cut	?	OUTSOURCE?
	OVERTIME	MGR approval	STAFF approval	CEO/Owner approval	
TRAVEL					
	TRAINING		50% CUT	DEFER	DEFER
	CONFERENCES		50% CUT	CRITICAL ONLY	DEFER
	CLIENT VISITS		20% CUT	DEFER	DEFER
	VENDOR VISITS		CNX	CNX	DEFER
	SALES	plus 10%	plus 20%	plus 50%	
MAINTENANCE					
	HOUSEKEEPING		15% CUT	consider internalizing	
	PLANT EQUIP		10% CUT		SAFETY ONLY
	BUILDING		40% CUT	DEFER	DEFER
	EXTERIOR		50% CUT	DEFER	DEFER
	....				

Source of Profit Addendum 2

The concentration on costs usually comes when there is a crises of revenue or profits.

Although we have learned the primary emphasis should be on sales (not costs) when profits are down, it also helps to have a *pre-planned system,* emphasis on *system,* for reducing costs when a drastic cut in quotes/sales/revenue happens.

Systematized cost cuts

A *system* of preplanned cost reductions, implemented when economic strife hits quickly.

Most cost reduction efforts are initiated when profits hemorrhage. When quotes drop (the prelude to poor profits), the urge to randomly and forcefully cut expenses takes over. It can devastate the long term health of the foundry/supplier because it is done in haste, without regard to history, and is usually based on one of these three (faulty) methods:

Percentages. Every department has to take a certain percentage budget hit. Although politically sound, it is fundamentally flawed. Why? Because some departments are critical in correcting the revenue defect. Do you want salespeople to make less calls?

Draconian measures. Designed solely to reduce expenses irrespective of their impact in the long run. Such as cancelling all employee travel and reducing customer service people or times.

General Sherman Survivalist Instincts-cut and burn techniques by those who know little of the processes. This is random destruction with no real methodology.

costs.

If the line drawn goes ***below the price baseline***, it indicates a belief that as costs are reduced, price should also be reduced.

If, by some fluke, the line drawn goes below costs, there is a gross misunderstanding of how to run a business... I would rethink this very closely.

Unbelievably

Many players will draw a line that parallels the cost line like railroad tracks. This indicates that price declines with costs. They are actually drawing the belief that lower prices will always get more sales, when in fact they have reduced the profit available and due.

Additionally, as price goes down, usually so does profit. It's very rare that the same amount (not percentage, a crucial point) of markup is applied.

Where you fall into one of these three (hopefully not the fourth) category will be an indicator as to how you view profit and where it originates.

Source of Profit Addendum 1

Do a self-evaluation

When I am invited to an onsite assessment, each of the leadership team is given a diagram like the one shown here.

The diagram shows the initial price charged for a casting product and also plots a hypothetical line of cost due to 'efficiencies'.
Participants are encouraged to look at the diagram and draw a line of their own which would show the price they would charge based on the plot of the costs.

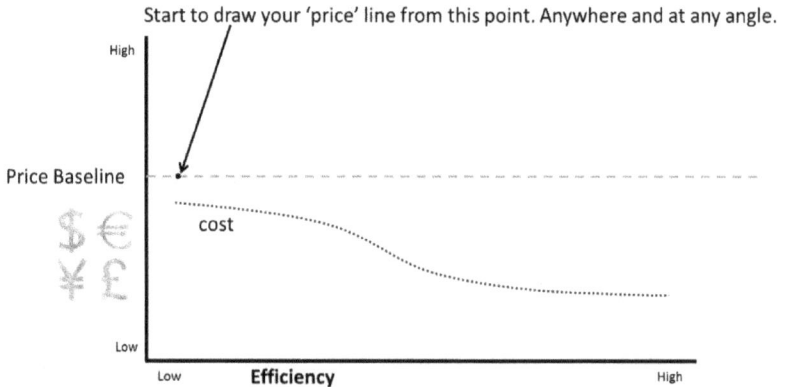

3 common answers

There are generally three responses:

If the participant's line *stays at the same price*, it shows astute recognition that cost reductions should be credited solely to the foundry as additional profit.

If the line goes *above the price baseline pre-printed* on the diagram, it indicates someone who realizes that price is completely independent of

Loyalty Myth Addendum

Why do <u>customers</u> leave?

In a well recited study some years ago, the metrics for why customers leave breaks out like this, modified for the B2B environment we live in:
- 1% change business forms and no longer need castings.
- 3% move away, consolidating operations elsewhere.
- 5% leave because of some type of social influence.
- 9% are persuaded by sales reps, other vendors, an offer, or other similar reasons.
- 14% of clients are dissatisfied with the service provided by the foundry.

So that about covers it, right?

But add up all the numbers and you quickly note this represents only 32% of the clients that left.

Why did the other 68%, the vast majority, leave?
- 68% of clients and customers leave because they didn't believe the business appreciated or cared about them. And they made that judgment based on service, flexibility, problem handling, lack of communication, and a general belief that they would be treated better elsewhere.

So the key to building loyalty is hard work. Overcome the myth by ensuring your clients know you, know you care, and know they are appreciated.

Do you have a Thank You *system*?

buyer, high quality. However, to a discerning metallurgist, maybe not so much...

Against a warranty or guarantee

This is a great tool to use to overcome the fluidity of high quality. The reason is that it substitutes solid backup (instead of mere standards and beliefs) that the buyer can hold the seller to.

Warranties and Guarantees are used throughout the business world but ignored in the metalcast industry. And to their loss. There are a savvy few who get it, and they reap the rewards of this simple tool.

Think about it. If a buyer is deciding between two quotes, and one has a guaranteed delivery date, which one do you think will have more weight? Obviously, if delivery on time is critical, you can draw the answer.

Although the other foundry may SAY they will deliver on time, the guarantee, which may have a price penalty, is more appealing.

It is like a small contract.

And it influences a LOT. While many will complain they could never guarantee anything, there are many areas that metalcasters could increase the 'quality' of the transaction through guarantees and warranties. And those who believe they will lose money are foolish and ignorant. Properly executed, I guarantee you will win more quotes than will ever be paid out in penalties.

So a warranty or guarantee will be judged as high quality along with just the castings.

Sorry, Charlie

While foundries believe that the published standard is the only guide, the other three factors can steal away your business. While many an engineer pines away for the day when buyers see things there way, others will realize the many ways high quality is judged by fallible (as opposed to engineers) people.

promised on time. And the invoice appears wrong. When they call the foundry, they aren't treated well. And have to call back several times because no one promptly returned their inquiry.

The quality of the actual castings only plays a minor role in this transaction.

And from the viewpoint of the buyer, it was not a high quality transaction. Subjective? Yes, absolutely.

But these are the points a buyer uses for the judgment of high quality. Thus, the metalcaster's assumption of high quality isn't actually true *in the mind of the buyer*.

> I remember raising my now-adult daughter through the teenage years. Any attempts at holding a standard was met with alternate proposals- just like the term 'high quality'. Maybe you have had a similar story from your kids.
>
> Remember the 'Be home by 11 PM'? Sounds pretty simple, doesn't it.
>
> If the definition was 'according to the clock on the mantle', that became a point of contention. Using the World Time website led to other issues- like the cellphone battery dying!
>
> My daughter eventually made it through teen years, but metalcasting businesses will always be stuck with different standards for high quality, just like the different interpretations of time in my daughter's life.

Against our needs or application

We use faucets every day. And my chrome or nickel plated faucets work great. I would call them high quality *for my needs*. Is this subjective? Absolutely. But is this a standard we all use? Absolutely.

So, although gold faucets are actually a higher quality, they are much more 'quality' than I need (or could afford!)

Some buyers accept castings that suit their specific needs. They are, to the

High Quality Myth Addendum

4 Ways to measure 'high quality'

There are at least four ways to judge quality in our circumstances. As engineers, we believe it is through science and processes. However, this is only a small part of the puzzle. Consider these other ways to measure quality:

Against a published standard

Whether an ISO rating, published ratings for specific alloys, or accepted standards of the industry, these are the 'objective' methods most preferred by engineers. They offer simple yes/no type solutions for comparison against a standard. It meets the standard or it doesn't. Black and white. No gray areas. An engineer's dream.
But not reality.

Against our own experience

In everyday life we make judgments based on our own experience. Someone may tout a product or service as excellent, but we quickly chime in with less than stellar experience as a counterpoint. How often have you heard or said:
- 'Well, from my experience…'
- 'That's not what happened to me…'
- 'I'm glad you had a good experience, because mine…'

Each of these are the counterpoint to high quality. And note that many are less than completely objective when you consider your own examples.
Castings are exactly the same. Let's look at why.

Consider a buyer who gets their castings late even though they were

metalcasting example.

Competing on your playing field

I consulted for a small TV shop that saw the threat of both Wall-Box and its cousin, the Everything Cheap Club. TV prices were obviously lower from both these competitors. What to do?

I live in Florida. We modeled the differences that the big boys could not offer. Consider the long list of benefits of dealing with the local guys that the Box stores couldn't offer:

- Delivery. Older people have smaller cars. TVs are only getting bigger…
- Setup. Besides the actual weight of the units, they are designed to be set up by engineers or your grandkids!
- Packing removal
- Programming the TV for the local cable, internet, or other service.
- Training on how to use the remote.
- 30 day in-home TV trial. Don't like it, apply the amount to any other TV.
- Local phone number for questions. No hard to understand foreign accents, no hours on hold.
- Personalized service.

The list goes on. And so did the business. They are still price sensitive, but there is a large niche of people who see the value of all the other services. Not everyone, of course.

Not everyone gets it

But you can't take the view of a friend of mine who ran a restaurant. He took me aside one day and jokingly announced "I'm a failure." When I asked why, he noted "Because I drove around last night and there are still people eating at home!"

Not everyone will use the foundry no matter how much value you offer.

But don't believe the 'We can't compete.' myth and just give up.

If you can't get over the hurdle, seek professional advice. There are people trained to overcome exactly this problem.

get the fee back for the full day consultation. (And, oh by the way, that guarantee differentiates me from every other consultant you have ever had onsite!)

Marketing has no ROI Myth

Any good leadership team always considers the Return on Investment (ROI) before the actual investment. This myth believes marketing is all smoke and mirrors and not subject the same scrutiny as any other financial venture.

But they're wrong.

Most have only dealt with Madison Avenue style 'branding' which has little or no place in this industry. And is, in fact, very difficult to measure its effectiveness.

But there are many ways to measure the effectiveness, called ROI, of any marketing effort. Including web site revisions, efforts to win new clients, or to increase quotes. A properly constructed effort can always be measured. (You may want to review Client Lifetime Value (CLV) to see this in action if you have doubts.)

If you can't measure the ROI of a marketing expenditure, I question whether it is effective use of capital. Sadly, many metalcasters and vendors do not know HOW to measure and therefore do not make the expenditure, I am not advocating against marketing and advertising budgets, but instead knowing how to ensure their ROI is assessed.

The "We can't compete with _____(fill in the blank)" Myth

You can personalize this myth easily. Fill in a country, a company, a niche, a product line, a geographical area, or a client market.

I have seen this same reaction among small businesses when 'Wall-Box' comes to town. Business people run in fear, screaming 'No one can compete with them!' Soon they have torches and clubs trying to stop their arrival.

But there are always a few who realize they can compete. How?

By doing what their new competitor cannot. Let's look at a non-

Sadly

Businesses who deal in commodities have the lowest profit margins and customer loyalty. Is this the kind of business you want to be in?

Even if a business believes it is a commodity, there are ways to separate from the crowd and thus break comparisons. Simply look on the grocery store shelves! Use milk for your research. The differentiations include size, type, additives, all-natural, organic, and other factors. And if you look carefully, many of those are surviving and thriving while charging premium prices.

Your metalcasting or supplier business can do the same.

Differentiation Myth

Almost the opposite of the commodity myth, this is a belief that 'if you build it, people will come'.

I heard a lecture during an American Foundry Society meeting that called most metalcasters 'order takers' instead of 'order makers'. Those who refuse to differentiate are order-takers. They wait for someone to call them to take an order.

As seen on…

Think of it like the person on the other end of the 800 number you call when you want to place an order for an item seen on TV. These people sit and wait for the phone to ring. (The difference, of course, is that someone else is out doing the marketing to MAKE the phone ring.) Order takers, on the other hand, sit and wait for the phone to ring without making themselves any different from their competitors.

Those who believe they cannot be differentiated also fall into this myth. They cannot see the differences, so assume there aren't any. They become like a commodity in everything they do.
And if you act like a commodity, you will be treated like one.

Anything can be differentiated. If you don't believe your business can, here is my challenge: I will bet my full day fee ($8000) that I can find 7 differentiating factors that you could use in your business. If I don't, you

Other Foundry Myths

Many myths can ultimately be traced to the primary 7 I have revealed. See if you see the thread which connects these to the primary Seven:

Commodity Myth

A subset of many of these myths is a belief that castings are a commodity. While many will deny this, their actions prove a deeply held belief that castings are indeed commodities.

Proof?

How do they show their belief in this myth?

-they are quick to lower prices, believing that this will attract more customers

-any reductions in costs means lower prices, thus reducing their profits automatically.

-they do nothing to differentiate their business, assuming (incorrectly) there is nothing different from any of their competitors, domestic or overseas

-their primary focus is on the product, not the customer. Like an auto gasoline advertisement, it's all about trying to convince users that their product is better.

-there is very little effort to retain and grade clients. Commodities survive because 'everyone needs them'. Like a dry cleaner, commodity-believing metalcasters assume quotes will just arrive and business will continue.

engineers and facilities.

Free mold/pattern with new order

When I speak at conventions and metalcasting gatherings, someone will always ask if lowering the price of the first order is a good idea to 'get the sale'.

In other industries this is called a *'loss leader'* approach. Entice the customers to buy an item you may lose money on, hoping they buy again or buy something else.

That's a fool's path in this industry.

Once you agree to sell at a low price, you have essentially locked in the price. It will be very challenging to raise your prices after the first order. And buyers will feel tricked.

Here is a rule you should never, Never, NEVER violate:

Never discount your main product.

Instead, *increase value using other incentives*.
In the foundry industry, a logical alternative is to swallow the cost of a new mold or pattern. If the client already has the mold, *free shipping to your foundry* is an easy way to kick up the value.

Any business can work with clients, see opportunities to help, and save customers time and money. The foundry business is no different. Except that few try.

Begin the transformation

These three methods (new clients, increasing quantity or increasing frequency) are the only way to increase revenue in a foundry.

Knowing that sales/revenue has three streams, you are beginning the journey of transformation from thinking like your competitors to being a shark in a school of sardines.

not see the possibility in their foundry and disregard the entire concept.

So read these examples *for concept only*.

Before sulking off to another chapter thinking 'that won't work in my foundry', consider how this same approach could be applied in your situation.

Money will gravitate to those who are innovative in the next 20 years. And any method that helps *buyers* look good will be rewarded.

Free weldment-to-cast evaluations

(NOTE: If you receive the **M4 SHORT SHEET** (see bonuses), you have seen this concept discussed already.)

Buyers are busy and not very pro-active. So when offered an evaluation that could make them look good, many will immediately bite the hook. They may forward the offer, allowing direct interface between you and their engineering or design team. No matter how they use it, an offer of free services will increase their stature and, if properly handled, will always result in additional sales for the foundry. (Even if the buyer never takes the free offer, the foundry still gets credit in the buyers mind simply for *making* the offer.)

Free 'parts count reduction' evaluations

Have you looked at the American Foundry Society's 'Casting of the Year' winners? Every year, either the winner, runners-up, or honorable mentions have submitted a cast which achieved significant parts count reductions for the buyer.

You can leverage this approach and actually *offer it as a service*. Every reduction in parts counts reduces the client's inventory, part number tracking, vendor risks, and should improve reliability and customer satisfaction.

Offered as part of a systematic approach, only C and D clients would ignore this opportunity.
Plus it gets the foundry's experts in the door to look around at all the ways improvements can be made using- you guessed it- the metalcaster's superb

The helpful friend

When a buyer is more than a customer, a trust is developed that plays out in increased quantities. When you are intimately familiar with clients, they respect the advice offered by the foundry team. This advantage allows your expertise to be part of their decision making. You become a helpful friend and advocate instead of just a vendor/supplier. Who else is offering cost saving advice? Who else is pointing out ways to increase their production? Your competitors don't.

Working closely with buyers and the client's design/engineering team can quickly identify these opportunities, too.

3. Get existing clients to buy more often (increased frequency)
The third method to increase revenue, and one routinely ignored, is to increase the frequency that buyers give you money. By increasing the frequency they buy, revenue increases.

If your 'A' clients are requesting quotes every 6 months and you entice them, through management of your people, products, performance and processes, to order every 5 months, you will see a significant revenue increase. (Mathematically, it's getting an extra order every 30 months.)

> *As a kid, I used to hand wash cars. After the melting winter slush had blackened their vehicle, I got the call. After a while, I found I could entice some of them for a cleaning so the car looked good for Mother's Day, earlier than they would usually get the car washed. Or after their summer vacation. They might not have called me, but I was there helping them, reducing their hassles, making their car (and them) shine.*

Can this work in a foundry? Only if you know your clients well. But those who establish relationships with their clients can see a large increase as the foundry becomes the trusted advisor.

Examples can be tricky

Since there are large, small, niched, generic, process specific, etc metalcasters, giving an example is dangerous. Why? Because a reader will

grading system.) And make sure they see this 'good client credit'. Remember that all buyers have short memories. Reminding them when they get a deal is very important and should be a part of every conversation.

A 'give back'

It can be a 'give-back' item that costs you nothing but is of value to buyers. If you would swallow the cost anyway, why not charge and then negotiate it away if necessary. Or offer it as a credit if the foundry screws up service, delivery, or in another area.

Use the fees to help move D clients

Have a 'D' client you want to move on? (Look at the Client Valuations section in the accompanying book if you are unsure what a 'D' client is.)

This fee will help! Apply the fees to D clients only. If it doesn't help them find another metalcaster, increase the fee until it does! If they still won't leave, at some point the extra profit will make up for their D status and keeping them isn't such a burden.

It's pure profit

In some plants, fees and surcharges alone could easily bring in $30K-$50K a year that could be used for any number of projects. *And it's all pure profit.*

Growth buying

Of course, the real money is in clients who buy more when they purchase. Why would they do that? Because you know them better than anyone else, can predict their needs, adapt your quote system to them, and offer services others can't or won't.

With growth buying, enticing your clients to buy more is a long term strategy born of a relationship. Know your clients, how they are using their castings, and you have opportunity.

and *growth buying.*

What is forced buying?

How do you force clients to 'buy' ie give you money?

Fees. Surcharges. Add-ons. Things like that.

For example, many foundries happily store the molds and patterns of their clients. At no cost. Sometimes for years before they are used.

Storage fee?

A simple fee might be charged for yearly storage; with a credit if the piece is used that year.

How many patterns does your facility store? Multiply that by almost any number, say $100, and how much could that generate?

The fee is small, so it is not economically feasible to move the patterns if the client doesn't like it. But large enough to increase revenue. And the money is *pure profit* since it is not a substitute for another revenue stream.

Surcharge?

Have a highly volatile cost, like energy? Keep your prices the same and implement an 'energy surcharge'. Raw materials? Consider an 'indexed raw materials surcharge'. None of this is dishonest, illegal, or even unethical. And it is very common in other industries. Even the government (ok, not a model of ethics…) adopts the phrase 'user fees' for certain areas instead of the less attractive 'new taxes'.

Look around and see what other opportunities you have to pass on costs.

Afraid to take a step like this?

You can still use it, even if it doesn't bring in a dime. Consider these ideas:

Turn the fee into a credit for good clients

You can institute a fee *and then waive it* for 'A' clients. (See Client Valuations in the companion book if you do not understand the A-D client

The simplicity will shock you.

There are only three ways

Here is the simple rule of revenue: **There are only three ways to increase revenue in a for-profit business.** Only three. (And most metalcasters only use one).

They are listed here and then covered in depth as you continue to read:
- Get more customers
- Get existing customers to buy more (quantity)
- Get existing customers to buy more frequently (shorter interval between quotes)

It's that simple. Now let's look at each in depth.

1. Get more clients or customers

You know my difference between customers and clients. If not, review it.

New clients seem to be the target everyone wants. Ad agencies will badger you to spend thousands of dollars to get new clients. The constant "We need more customers" is the perpetual refrain of most meetings about money.

So, other than the mistaken path of cutting costs alone (see the myth), getting new quotes from new customers is the road most metalcasters take, acting as if this is the only method. There is nothing wrong with new customers. Especially if you convert them to clients.

But they are the most expensive to acquire (ie higher acquisition or marketing costs) of the three ways to increase sales.

And there are two other methods, mostly ignored.

2. Get your existing clients to buy more (quantity) when they buy

I believe there are two subcategories in the metalcasting field that fall under this second revenue generating possibility. They are *forced buying*

The Source of Revenue Myth

> **Myth:** A Metalcaster needs new customers to increase the top line.
>
> **Fact:** There are other sources for quotes and revenue, many with lower acquisition costs than new clients.

The eternal chase

Walk into any sales meeting, almost anywhere in the world, and you will hear "We need more customers." It is a mantra driven by several factors, not the least of which is a misunderstanding the sources of revenue for a business –any business.

If you have heard me speak in person, you have already heard the difference between a client and customer. Read the Loyalty Myth section again if you don't know the difference.

Simplicity

Simplicity is the key to most systems and subjects. Sure, there are deep and abiding truths that are very intense. But the simple ones have the greatest long term impact.

In metalcasting, as in most businesses, the day to day running of the business can get complicated. But here again, stay on the simple track and everything else can become clear.

So let's name *ALL the sources of revenue, not just new customers.*

list should include absolutely ANYONE who has money for a casting.

Your life will be easier without them!

Recommend they go to a competitor who is willing to sacrifice their profit for the quote. Let your competitors deal with them. Competitors will go broke! The landscape is littered with the carcasses of companies who believed (1) everyone was a potential client and (2) lowering prices to get more orders was a long term viable solution.

Breaking the myth

The key to breaking this myth is to ensure that your team delivers so much value that a buyer would be nuts (and, admittedly, some are!) to accept anyone else's quote. And the best time to make the case is when courting a new client or quoting an existing one.

Note: if want to read about the argument that buyers are paid to buy only on price, read the addendum. Everyone who already 'gets it' can move on...

Notes
[1]Dan S Kennedy, *No BS Price Strategy*, Dan S Kennedy and Jason Marrs , pg   81-82.

When Prices are the Same

If all prices are the same, like our second chair example, the *value* option kicks in quickly. This is the second video.

Price is only one of several variables and may not be the deciding factor. It may have an influence, but may not even be the dominant variable.

Proof in your foundry

Proof of this concept lies right in your foundry.

Have you had customers who willingly paid a premium for faster service? This is a perfect example where delivery time is much more important than price. You actually raised the price and the buyer accepted it because of the value they received.

Are you beginning to see why this is a myth-perception?

You do the same

Your personal behavior mirrors industrial buyers because both of you are humans. (Ok, wild assumption, but give the buyers the benefit of the doubt.)

If offered three cars as described below, which would you buy?
- ✓ 'As new' YUGO (look it up) for $19,000.
- ✓ New American made 4-door sedan for $20,000.
- ✓ New top of the line Mercedes® for $22,000.

Everyone picks the Mercedes (well, there may be a Yugo fan out there I guess...), not because of price but because of VALUE. Perceived value. Anyone choosing the lowest price (buying only on price) would be considered a fool. The gap between the lowest price and the highest value is so apparent, few pick anything else.

And the same thinking applies to industrial buyers.

Let them go!

Lastly, if a company *only* chooses on price, you don't want them! They are D clients (see the Numbers book). Get out of the thinking that your client

Whose fault is that? (You won't like the answer!) Hint: Not the buyers!

This is the foundry's fault. Once the buyer *knows* the differences, if they ignore the value and buy only on price, it is their fault.

But if a business acts like a commodity, they will be treated as a commodity by their customers.

Get out your smart device

TheAuthorSpeaks®

Scan the code to listen or go to
http://bit.ly/1xCp6aD

TheAuthorSpeaks®

Scan the code to listen or go to
http://bit.ly/1pr1WMh

These two short 'lessons' show the difference in typical buying based on either price or value.

In one, diagrams are used to show what happens when the value is considered equal across all products- a commodity.

The second shows how buyers think when prices are very close or the same.

When Perceived Value is the Same

If the *perceived value of all choices is the same*, such as in the first office chair example, the purchase decision is made on price alone. But it is *not* a price decision. Do not be deceived.
It is a value decision with price being the only variable.

That should be repeated and reread.

It is a value decision with price being the only variable.

In your purchase, you noted (possibly only subconsciously) there were no other points of differentiation. Every chair was the same, no differences in vendor, billing, delivery, or customer service- anything. So the only value proposition was built on a different price.

But you didn't actually buy solely on price.

And this is *not* semantics.

The rejected bids, the suppliers you did not choose, were based on value, and *price was the sole point of differentiation* in determining that value. If the losing office supply houses think this is a 'buy on price' story, they are wrong. Let's look further to understand why.

Let's change the scenario

Back to no chairs in the office, tired feet, and phone calls.

This time you get three chair quotes, again of the same style, fabric, and color.

But one of the suppliers guarantees his delivery schedule and time, warrants the chair against defects for 2 years, offers on-site setup with packing removal, and a certificate for 50% off any lamp to allow you to read while sitting in the chair.

Now you have *factors other than price* on which to make a decision. If all the prices were the same, you would probably pick the best value- the one with all the extras.

And most people, including industrial buyers, would pay a small premium for the additional value.

Price is only one of several variables in any decision.

Who's at fault?

Castings are not clearly differentiated in the mind of a buyer. Since most buyers assume all castings are equal (you haven't told them anything different!) they choose on price. They come to believe castings are a commodity.

"*Price* is never an issue unless *value* is unclear"

It works in your personal life, and also works in business. If you find your clients are basing their decision solely on price, your *value proposition, the value of doing business with you, is unclear.*
Buyers only buy on price when there are absolutely no other cues on which to make a decision.

Example

Put your *'I am a buyer'* hat on for a minute. Let's use an example of price versus value.
You have a new office. But no place to sit. Your feet ache from standing. A LOT. But there are no chairs. You MUST sit down. So you call office furniture stores and ask them to quote your chair requirements.

Three stores each quote the *exact same chair*. Same style, color, fabric. No difference in customer service, billing, or delivery. The only difference is the price.

Which one would you choose?

With no discernable difference, price is the only variable and so, obviously, you choose the one with the lowest price.

The myth begins

After sitting down in your new chair (AAAAAAHHHHH), the phone rings. It's a sales rep from one of the office supply houses asking why they didn't get the order. You tell them, quite frankly, because the supplier you used had a lower price.

Know what is happening at the other end of the phone?

The rep hangs up and sulks. "Everyone only buys on price," he concludes.

But wasn't price the sole decision?

Not at all. If everyone had offered different chairs at different prices, you would not have chosen on price alone because there were *differences other than price you had to consider.*

competitive price, and over half of that 20% occurs within the context of pre-framed competitive bidding. The other 80% of the purchases are made based on more complex criteria."[1]

And that more complex criteria is the rest of the variables in the value equation.

Only C and D Clients truly buy on Price Alone

In the B2C or consumer world, the only people buying solely on price are those forced by their economic circumstances. They have no other choice.

It is the same with individual buyers in a B2B environment. The only ones who ignore value and only buy on price are forced by their circumstances.

You don't want them as clients.

If you look in the Numbers book, part of this Limited Edition, this is where Client Grading comes in. Buyers who select only on price, in spite of obvious value differences, are C and D clients.

They have no loyalty and will drop you over $100. Or haggle you down to meet a competitor's price.

Either way you lose.

And if they can't see the value in what you do, don't ever expect referrals, case studies, or other revenue building extras.

Except for the Ignorant Ones

ALL industrial buyers, except the ignorant ones, buy on value. Think of it. Why would they risk their job buying solely on price when there is a distinct value difference? The truth is all buyers select a vendor/supplier based on value. Price is an essential, but not sole element, in the decision.

UNLESS there are no other indicators of value.

Wall Poster

Print this on your wall in large font:

How can it be a myth?

I actually use the term misperception. The reasoning is simple.

In many cases, buyers actually do only buy on price!

But the *reason* is not what you think.

They buy on price only because there are no other cues to establish value.

Read that sentence carefully.

They buy on price *only* because there are no other cues to establish value.

Until you understand why buyers are only using price as a decision point, you are convinced that price is the ONLY decision point.
But all buyers are human and actually buy on *value*.

This is significantly different from price alone. Price is a component of value, but for most buying decisions, it is one of a number of points to be considered.

What's actually happening?

People buy on value. And price is one component of value. But there are others, including customer service, convenience, color style, reputation- the list is almost endless and different for each purchase and buyer.

When people are perceived to be buying on price alone, that means they have isolated the price variable by itself and assumed all the other parts of the value decision are the same among all the choices.

This happens mostly in commodities.

Research, anyone?

This is more than guessing, intuition and psychology games. Outside research with solid numbers confirms the myth:

"The reality of B2B commerce is that only about 20% of all purchases made by professional purchasing agents, other executives or managers, authorized department heads, and business owners are based on lowest

Unlike the myth of our discussion.

But the points are the same.

How do Myths begin?

Myths get started from actual, but misinterpreted, experience.

The Buy On Price myth reminds me of a great story that uses the same principles.
Jessica was learning to cook. She and her mother were preparing a roast for dinner. Her mother explained 'you always cut two inches off the end of the roast and cook it separately.'

When Jessica questioned this odd step, her mother told her "I never thought about it. That's what my mother taught me. Call your grandmother and ask."

The little girl called, asking the reasoning behind the 'cut off two inches' step. Grandmother didn't have an answer either, as this is the way she had been taught by <u>her</u> mother. Since her mother was still alive, she encouraged Jessica to call her great-grandmother Janie for an explanation.

Great grandmother Janie had been cooking forever and still lived at home. As Jessica explained her quest, and told of all the generations that had been doing this funny step without reason, Janie laughed heartily.

"It's really very simple, Jessica. You see, when I was teaching your grandmother to cook a roast, we had to cut two inches off the end because the roasting pan I owned was so small!"

It's really a misperception

This myth persists because it is perceived to be constantly reinforced.

> **MYTH:** The majority of buyers accept quotes based solely on price. Lowest price always wins the quote. There are few exceptions.
>
> **Fact:** Many metalcasters see competitors win quotes and assume price is the only reason they were not chosen. This is a false conclusion that doesn't fit the facts.

'Buyers Only Buy On Price' Myth

Of all the myths discovered in analyzing closed metalcasters, this one was the second most pervasive. And the myth is not exclusive to them. It can easily be heard throughout the industry. You may have heard it or even used that as an excuse for losing a quote.

History is replete with examples of misinterpretation like this: Real data but wrong conclusion. It results from an incomplete understanding of what is actually being observed.

Believe in Santa?

Think of it this way. What reinforced your belief in Santa Claus?
- it was generally accepted by all your peers
- it was reinforced in the 'industry'
- there were examples available to see (his 'assistants')
- there was the actual 'evidence' on Christmas

Yet, in spite of all this, we know (many of us, at least!) that Santa is a myth. Based in some historical reality, but a myth that endures. Yes, it is harmless.

Consider two quotes, one that just agrees to all the requirements along with a price and payment terms. The other also includes several of the tools in this list, guaranteed on-price/on-time delivery. Which would you choose? Buyers will do the same.

One last example

Did an on-site consultation with a metalcaster who operated debt free. That is huge to some buyers, indicating internal business strength and reliability. Yet this information was not explained in every quote- or anywhere for that matter.

Foundry management took it for granted instead of leveraging it-providing the information for comparison to their competitors. A statement such as "XYZ foundry has zero debt. What does that mean to you? Any foundry carrying a debt load is under the risk of failure with a slight turn of the economy, foreign competition, or labor issues. When you deal with us, that threat is entirely eliminated. Have you had an order with a metalcasting house that suddenly closed- leaving you in the lurch? Banish that thought with XYZ foundry. Be sure to compare this factor with our competitors..."

Used as a comparison tool, trust building, or as education, it is a buyer oriented metric that can be leveraged against competitors. There are many examples like this if you only look...

Myth Busted?

A quote system isn't really necessary. None of the foundries that closed had one. It's only a requirement for those metalcasters who want a stable business over the long run. With great clients. Good profit margins. And for those who want to grow the business. And survive and thrive through economic hassles like 2009-2011.

And it all starts with a Quote System that smashes through the myth.

Compare your 'promised' versus 'actual' delivery times historically. If the latest delivery metric averaged 3 days late, adjust promised delivery time for each quote by adding *FIVE* days.

> *As a management advisor, there are some areas where I guarantee my work. No results? Pay nothing. In other areas, my paid subscription newsletter, the "UGLY Marketing Newsletter for Metalcasters and Suppliers", has a 20X guarantee. If you implement the ideas in the newsletter and have not received at least 20 times the cost of the newsletter in a year's time, I will refund the subscription price AND continue it for another year free. (Contact Debby@TheFoundryMarketer.com for more info.)*

Then put a 'kicker' into the quote. "If we fail to deliver by the promised date, we agree to an automatic credit of 1% per day for every day it is late, *to be applied to the next order*".

This accomplishes several things:

- eliminates fears that you don't really care about the delivery time
- gives them a financial compensation credit against *another order* which means they have to order again to use the credit!

The risk is almost zero to the foundry because you modified your delivery date to account for your typical late delivery times. But the buyers will see it as a risk reduction, trust building, guarantee. It won't be their butt on the line if you are late. They will look good to their management for having 'negotiated' this late delivery deal. And even if you are late, they would have to be pretty upset to *not* use the credit for another order!

Accountability options relieve the buyer's stress. That makes your quote look better.

Do I need to do all that?

Not at all. But I'll bet you are doing nothing right now. Pick one or two and start using those tools. Then watch the reaction- and the results.

Put on your Buyer Hat

Kenmore appliances, DieHard batteries, Craftsman tools. That phrase is now the most commonly used guarantee throughout retailing, including online.

I remember as a teenager, working at a local Sears store. A gentleman bought a lawnmower. I put it in his trunk. It was in a box with the handle folded down over the main body. The next day, the man returned, requesting a refund. I went to his car to find the mower still in the box, but the box smashed! I asked what happened. The customer told me he had been rear-ended taking the mower home. But since the sign said, 'Satisfaction Guaranteed or Your Money Back', he wanted a refund.

And he got it!

How can you build trust without risking everything?

One of the easiest is **Guarantees** and **Warranties.**

Anything can be guaranteed. You can be creative here and guarantee something you take for granted- but the buyer doesn't. For example:

"ZZZ foundry guarantees your castings will meet spec. If not, we will re-cast them at no charge and ship them priority express."

You already do this, right? So why not make it a trust building *guarantee*?

Warranties are rarely used in metalcasting. You can use them and stand out. Could you warranty a casting for 2 years? Why not? If it is designed and poured properly, it should easily last that long. If not, there is a problem. Or you can warranty the fit for a subassembly. Again, if the foundry did their homework, this is almost zero risk. But it builds a tremendous bank of trust.

Accountability Options

In your business there are many areas where you can shift the risk, and build trust, by assuming accountability *in writing*. Here is an example:

Guarantee your delivery time. (Sounds scary, doesn't it? Lots of variables you can't control...)

How to do that without getting burned?

to your advantage.

In most cases, this is not a discussion of eutectic temperatures. The format should include the features and benefits you take for granted but are *important to the buyer*. You may want to review the section in the companion book on Client Oriented Metrics.

New Buyer Visits

However, you also have an opportunity to make a deep and lasting impression. One US foundry told me of their quarterly onsite training sessions for new buyers. Do you think travelling to a new city, being hosted by a foundry, and seeing castings formed, up close and personal, makes an impression on new buyers? They will always remember that foundry!

A book

As a multiple published author, I can assure you a book is much easier than it has ever been. A short paperback (or hardcover if you really want to impress) can have a lasting impression and also become a desktop reference. *"How to Buy the Highest Quality Sand Castings in the Midwest US for the Least Hassle- Guaranteed"* (made up title) authored by the metalcaster's team makes a great giveaway for less than $10-$15. And every time it is referenced, it brings your foundry, staff, and castings to mind.

Other ways to educate
There are also White Papers, Case Studies, published papers, testimonials from others, webinars, and teleseminars. Plus many others.

#3 Trust Building/Eliminating Risk

Quotes, and a quote *system,* are a great place to eliminate risk, which builds trust.

Remember 'Satisfaction Guaranteed or Your Money Back'? The Sears company started this policy almost 100 years ago to build trust in their brand. This simple statement shifted the risk for their entire product line on themselves completely. And it worked. It made Sears a trusted brand.

#1 Differentiation

Comparing apples to apples is important at times. But not in your quote. A well designed quote system should make it nearly impossible to compare your quote with competitors.
Your quote should be so different from competitors that it is comparing apples to oranges. Or, if you work closely with me, you will have heard this as 'Apples-to-Unicycles" comparison. Apples *can't* be compared to unicycles…

Throughout your life, there are things that are the absolute best; that defy comparison. This is where we get the English word 'incomparable' from. It is not compare-able, there is nothing to compare it to.

Your metalcasting business should be on the same wavelength. Done properly, using differentiation, you can build this aura about your business. One place to start is with the quote, which should emphasize all the services, capabilities, and other factors that others do not offer. Or better yet, can't offer.

Even a simple sheet which notes your capabilities and those of your competitors. But using capabilities *from the buyer's perspective*.

Like what?

Frame your comparisons to the buyer's needs.

"Our *onsite metallurgist* ensures your specs are met the first time, saving you time, hassles *and* money."

"Our award winning design team will review your spec to identify opportunities *to save you short term money in the casting process*, and identify *long term savings* with economical design alternatives."

"Our weekly communications assure you of progress *without having to call us*. While others keep you on hold, tell fibs big and small, we keep you constantly updated to help you sleep better at night."

#2 Education

Many buyers are poorly educated about your team, your metalcasting business, and actual castings. Each one is a huge area that can be leveraged

That closure put a whole group of buyers on report with their boss, made them scramble for an alternate source, and ruined their trust in the casting business.

"Fool me once, it's your mistake, but fool me twice, it's mine." These burned buyers will remember- and become even more suspicious in dealing with the industry.

The less *YOU* are a hassle to deal with, the *MORE* they build trust, confidence, and affinity.

So what do you do?

The perfect way to handle this is with a quote system that identifies each buyer's needs and fills them. Whether it be a need for education, assurance, hand-holding, decision making guidance, or trust building.

Every quote system needs to be flexible, with different tools to handle different tasks. Imagine a surgeon arriving in the operating room with only a scalpel and scissors. For every operation, no matter the type. Or a golf professional hoping to win the Masters with only a driver and a putter. Each must use different tools for the challenges they face at the moment.

Yet metalcasters everywhere use a single, unsharpened tool, hoping to win millions of dollars of business.

What tools are the minimum?

What tools form the foundation of a quote system? The following is a minimum; aggressive business owners will have many more. You will see a lot of overlap. Just as it takes several tools for any mechanic to fix a problem, so it is here. The problem is convincing a wary, untrusting buyer. How many implements does it take?   Whatever is needed to fix the problem ie win the quote!!

Let's look closer at a minimum toolbox that every metalcaster should have handy:

Then, there are mature or educated buyers who understand what you do, possibly even how you do it. They are loyal to some degree, but have doubts in certain areas. They know the lingo, the insider's words.

Like a comfortable friend that you have dated for a long time.

Your long term, 'A' client buyers are loyal, trusting, know the system and how to work with you. They get it. They put up with more but you also value them more. They need a completely different style of communication that buttresses their status and importance.

Like those couples who seem to endure no matter the challenges.

All the same?

Yet, most metalcasters treat all three "partners" the same. Would you share at the same level on a first date? Or act differently after a yearlong relationship has been built? Or have different expectations after being married for several years?

So why would all quotes follow a simple online form? Yet it happens in many foundries.

Treating all buyers the same doesn't work out well… the relationship may endure, but it won't thrive.

What do buyers really want?

A hassle free, on spec, on price, on-time delivery. They want castings. And a whole lot more!

They want anything that eliminates their risk of dealing with your foundry, since they have been burned in the past. They want anything that makes their job easier, makes them look good to their boss, gets them out of work on time, doesn't keep them up at night.

"58 year old foundry closes"

Scary headline to a buyer. Do you think they closed after fulfilling everyone's order? Shipping their customer's patterns and molds to other foundries? Completing all customer's requirements? HA!

In talking to a metalcaster, he was frustrated that incoming prospects wouldn't fill out the two page form properly on his website when requesting information. They wouldn't give email addresses, phone numbers, time of day to call, weight and size of the castings, alloy, delivery date, etc.

I asked why he needed two pages of information to initiate a relationship and he just stared at me.

"That's the way our system works," he snorted.

Imagine going into a tire store and asking for a quote for tires, only to be told to fill out a form full of personal data. "I only want some information..." you plead.

"That's the way our system works!" replies the clerk.

You can stand on your horse and scream at people or you can choose to interact with them- and get their confidence, trust, and dollars- by understanding their needs instead of yours.

Loyalty

There is some with your son, more with your daughter, and enough loyalty to put up with you from your spouse.

Building the loyalty factor into quotes is done using several methods. Once established, client loyalty is pretty durable. It will take a lot to break. A well designed quote system has built in triggers to build loyalty.

Buyers and relationships

There are new buyers who do yet have a strong relationship, have no trust built, and no experience to rely on. They have approached you but also approach your competitors. There is no loyalty. They don't know how your system works, yet.

Like looking at matches on a dating site.

Maturity

The maturity of the relationship is pretty thin for a 3 year old. Your spouse is much more trusting, understands your foibles, and communicates on a completely different plane. These same characteristics occur with new buyers, those who have little experience, and those you have cultivated over years together.

Communication skills

Your young son, teenage daughter, and spouse have different skillsets. So it is with non-engineer buyers, technical buyers, and trained engineers, PEs and buying teams. You accomplish the most when your communication is tailored to the audience, even an audience of 1.

Familiarity with the 'system'

Your son understands yes and no, more than that is confusing or misunderstood. The 18 year old is learning to push the envelope and develop a life of her own. Your spouse gets the big picture in most decisions. (Or makes them!) These are based on 'knowing the system' in which you operate.

Buyers are at different levels and should be approached from that perspective to ensure they are most comfortable with you as a business and advocate for their needs.

Trust

Your 3 year old may not trust you will catch him when he jumps from the side of the pool at your urging. The 18 year old may trust you for that, but may not trust you for the guidance in other parts of her life. Your spouse trusts you implicitly, even when there are questions. (Hey, I believe in perfect marriages, ok??)

Once trust has been developed in a business relationship, the communication is much easier. The trust building principles incorporated into your quote system for new, untrained, or seasoned buyers can leverage the position in the relationship. Emphasizing on-time and on-cost delivery is more important to a new-to-you buyer than a long time client.

The Quote System Myth

> Myth: "A quote is a quote is a quote. Everyone is just a customer, so all quotes are done the same way."
>
> Fact: People are different, and buyers are people. A quote system that uses this 'inside baseball' knowledge will increase quote acceptance, profits, and stability.

Everyone is the same? Really?

You don't communicate the same to different members of your family, why should you communicate the same to every buyer? They are human and each is different. And in a different relationship with you. Just like family. (Which can be good or bad!)

Are buyers really different?

Quoting differently to different clients is the touchy feely part that annoys most engineers. It is the *relationship*. That is what buyers really want. So think of it in these terms:

Would you talk to your 3 year old son the same as your 18 year old daughter and the same to your spouse of 20 years? Of course not. Each one requires a different level of communication.

Here are 5 central factors that affect the foundry's relationship and change the communication paradigm between buyers:

myth becomes active when costs are cut merely to accommodate the current level of sales. (see the video)

Believers will say 'we cut costs to increase profits'. That is the first time the myth rears its head. You see, there are no profits in costs. (Have I said that before?)

There is no profits possible unless there are quotes/sales/revenue.

How is a quote computed? Simplistically, it is fixed costs + variable costs + profit = quote. Sure this is simplistic, but accurate. Every expenditure is either fixed or variable. Assuming (HUGE word in this context) the accuracy of fixed and variable costs, profit is added to make the quote.

Bottom Line

This short section has one purpose. To help re-orient leadership's thinking about the balance between costs and profit. To emphasize that quotes need to be the focus when there is a defect in sales and revenue, not costs. Control costs, but emphasize increasing the quantity of quotes accepted, the quality of the clients, and the value you offer. This is the solution to increased profitability.

Take the test to see how you view the relationship between costs and price in the Addendum to this section.

> ## What about Efficiency changes?
>
> *As I travel and speak, there is always someone, unswayed by facts, trying to re-affirm his or her belief in the myth. In all those conversations, there has only been one justification that has partial merit.*
>
> *If an efficiency is introduced, won't this increase profits?*
>
> *This could be true but only when two points are recognized.*
>
> *1. Efficiencies cost money. Better equipment. Better processes. Even realigning work stations to reduce labor still costs money. If the cost can be paid back in less than 6-12 months, it is probably worth the investment. But point #2 is the most critical.*
>
> *2. Efficiencies must be credited to the foundry, not reduce the quote prices. Most metalcasters eagerly reduce their margins and profits when they reduce costs by also reducing prices. This nullifies the efficiency unless it can be proven they sold more castings to make up for the profit shortfall.*
>
> *And I have NEVER seen that computation done!*
>
> *But 'lower prices always sells more' is another myth...*

reducing costs.

Don't forget

There is one critical assumption in the Source of Profit myth. Costs must already be controlled. By themselves. Not in relation to anything else. *The*

> I worked for a super high end transportation provider who saw profits plummet during a downturn. New management was brought in that had only dealt with commodities. Their only answer was to cut costs. Not increase sales. The impact was immediate. The company was now 'profitable'.
>
> But the long term effect was disastrous.
>
> Short term profits destroyed the client base by losing their trust, and angered the employees. The assets were deteriorating, service was rapidly falling, clients were leaving for competitors. But, hey, they showed a profit!

Visionary vs Bean Counter

There are two major leadership styles in today's corporate environment. One is the entrepreneurial visionary. The other the bean counter.

Yes, this sounds like a slam to the second group. Believe me, I know that neither one of these can be the sole way to run a company over the long term. The visionary will outspend the company and the bean counter will ruin a brand through senseless cuts. Obviously, a balance is needed.

Each side actually represents the two ways to view the Source of Profit Myth.
The visionary knows there are no profits unless there are quotes. This is the critical distinction in the myth. There are no profits in costs.

The bean counter believes all the profits are in reducing costs.

There is a great book, *"Car Guys vs Bean Counters"*, about the former leviathan General Motors. The author, Bob Lutz, was a senior executive and recalls the way metrics and studies were used to continually cut costs until people essentially stopped buying their cars. Now, obviously, not everyone stopped. But enough did to almost bankrupt the company. It's a great read, and I highly recommend the book. You don't have to be a vehicle manufacturer to get the point.

GM had lost sight of the fact that profits were dependent on sales, not on

Read the…

Source of Revenue Myth if necessary. There are multiple ways to increase income. And every 'sale' has profit built into the process. Every increase in income has both a contribution to costs as well as profit.

A simplified view

Looking at diagrams may not help re-organize your thinking. But maybe examples will do it. Consider these two:

When you open a foundry, you already have costs. Let's assume yearly costs of $1M before a single sale. If there is not a single sale, costs are still part of the business. Cut those costs to $500K and there is still no profit. You MUST have sales to have profits because profits only reside in sales.

Now, using the same scenario above, you have $1M in overhead. You make a sale. The sale price was composed of variable costs, fixed costs, and profit. (Simplistic but true). The sale was for $100K of castings. Sales have profits built into them. In this case, the costs were larger than the sales-generated profit.

Although, in this example, management could lower costs below 100K, and thus unmask the profit, we know the fixed costs are much higher. It is possible to lower costs to show a profit, but it will devastate the company.

What happens when

The only time reducing costs can expose profits ('increase' has the wrong connotation) is:

- when costs are not properly controlled to begin with

OR

- the sale price does not have an adequate profit built into it

OR

- when service, customer support, training, or other long term brand differentiators are cut.

another more lucrative job.

He gave up the car which now limits his ability to accept overtime or even be on time for work.

The cheaper apartment's location, combined with the bus requirement, adds 2 unproductive hours to the daily schedule.

And the boss is not happy that he is not available via phone.

Cutting costs may not be the answer. *Controlling* costs smartly always is.

A business comparison
If a business is cutting costs to make a profit, they also risk making the same mistake as an individual.

Too many CEOs and owners ignore the 'increase revenue' solution. So they cut costs in areas that have a decidedly negative impact on long term profits

They eliminate marketing and advertising.

And reduce sales staff. (This is especially surprising since most outside sales people, even in this industry, are commission based.)

Cut customer/client support staff.

Shorten customer support hours.

They eliminate engineering staff that supports clients.

Lay off plant workers to the point product is now late.

Double up tasks with remaining employees to the point customer calls are not returned.

The worst I have seen (no kidding) is calling a metalcaster only to have the phone immediately go to 'we can't come to the phone right now, please leave a message at the tone…' And this was at 10 AM.

In this example, like the personal story, costs were cut to accommodate the level of sales. That can be a dangerous situation.

This is a great analogy, but there is a significant part missing for companies where the profit margin is low even with adequate costs controls.

A family example

The 'live within your means' advice has sustained generations of families. It simply implies that your expenses should be less than what you earn. Pretty simple.

If you earn, after taxes, $5000 a month, the prudent person should be spending, in monthly living expenses, less than that. Of course, if you are more conservative, you want to spend less than 90% of that figure to ensure at least 10% goes to savings. The ultra-conservative, like me, also allocate 10% for helping others through donations, charity, or other methods.

But the concept is basically sound.

But it's missing an essential point. Reducing personal expenditures is certainly one way to make the equation work. So is ***increasing income!***

To increase the mathematical difference between my living expenses and income, most people ignore the increasing income answer. This may be working longer hours, overtime, holidays, extra shifts, getting a raise or a promotion. All of these will also improve the bottom line.

Family example gone wrong

The problem arises when we ignore the second method or income cure.

Imagine a person who must continually cut costs to meet the goal of 'living within their means'.

To make ends meet, he or she shuts off the phone/cell phone, sells the car in favor of riding the bus, drops the night classes, and moves to a cheaper apartment that is much farther from work.

While this will, hypothetically, allow him to live within his means, consider the long term as well as short term impact.

He gave up night classes which could lead to a raise or promotion or

Source of Profit Myth

> **Myth**: A business is simple. If I reduce costs, I increase profits. Therefore, in time of reduced sales, emphasizing reduced costs is the answer to increased long term profits.
>
> **Fact**: There are no profits in costs. The only transaction that brings in profits is sales. Costs need to be *controlled*. But the key to profits is *additional sales, and should always take priority over randomly reducing costs.*

More than any other myth, this is the most difficult to understand. You may have to read this section several times. It is not a semantic argument. It is a philosophical re-orientation to recognize the importance of sales over costs alone. This is an especially important section for anyone who believes the key to profit is **only** (important word) cost reductions and controls.

Business people who believe this myth are usually called 'bean counters'.

Why is this a myth?

A misunderstanding of what is actually occurring on a profit and loss statement leads to this myth. Using simple math, lowering costs appears to 'increase profit'. But this is a gross misinterpretation of what is actually occurring and what needs to be done to cure defects in sales and revenue.

I read an article where the writer used the phrase 'living within your means' to describe why some businesses fail to make an adequate return.

examples:

- Service life, shelf life, pressure capacity, corrosion resistance
- Replacement priority, misuse or mistake on customer's part, conformity to provided drawings
- Price, delivery schedule, customer service, country of origin

In summary

Don't take offense reading the title of the chapter. No one is saying your products, your company's products, are low quality.

When everyone is perceived to be the same, there is no difference. If metalcasters are perceived as a commodity, quality is not only assumed, but is the minimal ticket to get into the arena. And since the word 'high' can only be used in a relative fashion (higher than *WHAT?*) the term itself has become clouded to the point of being meaningless.

Implement the ideas here and you can still use the term, but in a way that influences buyers and brings in more quotes.

NOTE: If you want to understand the logic that keeps the myth alive, read the addendum at the back of this book. There is a second addendum that explains four common methods for determining quality- from a buyer's perspective.

Notes
[1] Harvard Business Review, January-February 2013, "Rethinking the 4 P's" by Richard Ettenson, Eduardo Conrado, and Jonathan Knowles

Remember these are historical. They are a summary of other's actual experience. They can include:

- On time Delivery
- On cost delivery
- On spec delivery
- Buyer rejection rate
- Buyer failure rate
- Client average time with foundry
- And a whole lot more!

Read the section on COM in the companion book.

Buyers interpret the data as 'high quality' because these are facts and numbers that directly affect them. (Few of your competitors will use these, and fewer understand them.)

Guarantees and Warranties

If you believe the foundry's products are indeed superior to all others, you need to back that up with more than words. And science and metallurgy won't always cut it. The solution is a guarantee or warranty.

Does that make you immediately afraid?

If so, it's because there is always risk. But every risk has reward. Why does it make you tremble in fear? I would bet you are concerned:

- The warranty or guarantee will get abused
- You have no idea if the product will indeed support the warranty or guarantee.
- You don't know what to guarantee

I *never* recommend a warranty or guaranty IF you honestly do not believe in the product. But if you do, this is the primary ways to brag about 'high' quality. And it can be very fruitful in your quotes because few metalcasters ever warrant their castings.

What can you guarantee/warranty?

Almost everything. Both products as well as services. Here are a few opinion can easily influence. An *experience* can be 'high quality', which washes over to the actual engineering behind the product- good or bad.

Imagine staying at a 5 star hotel. But you are treated poorly, the sink is clogged, and the TV remote doesn't work. Your sleep is interrupted by street noises. And in the morning, while you are trying to sleep, you get 'KNOCK, KNOCK,KNOCK- HOUSEKEEPING!!'

While someone else judged the hotel to be 5 stars, would you say it was 'high quality'? Probably not.

Pretty unscientific but realistic in today's social media driven world.

What others say about you

Using testimonials and Case studies is highly regarded in B2B circles. And leverages opinion and experiences into 'high quality'. When other speak highly of you, it has more credence, more believability.

You can orchestrate this.

Testimonials are other buyer's positive comments. Do you have a system to solicit testimonials? Many metalcasters claim they receive most of their new business by referrals, but few actually have a system to solicit testimonials, the first step in a referral process.

Case Studies are examples where your team solved a client's problem. It is specifically written so readers conclude 'if it worked for them, it will work for me' and choose you as their casting supplier.

Obviously, those who give testimonials and agree to Case Studies believe they had a high quality experience/product. Readers perceive that, too.

Making it personal

Client Oriented Metrics (COM) is discussed in the accompanying book. This is a metric summary of the experience of others as documented by the foundry. A forward looking and thinking metalcaster uses this data to show high quality. How?

COM allows you to sway the buyer using metrics they care about: metrics that demonstrate dealing with the foundry makes their life easier.

Recognized System

If the foundry has qualified under a recognized system, say an ISO9000 Quality Standard, that should be an important element of the discussion with potential clients.

But you may have to explain it to them. Does the buyer recognize the advantages of certification? Do they really know what it means? And what it means *to them*? Remember they only want a casting. Your in-house stuff has little meaning to them unless they recognize, understand, and TRUST the differences you show.

So, unless you are dealing with the government or some other organization that REQUIRES the certification, it holds little weight for the 'high' in high quality when compared to competitors.

To ensure your certification is viewed in your favor may take education. If a certification ensures you can cast with fewer defects, the buyer could care less. On the other hand, if it ensures lower prices, longer (guaranteed) service life, or other 'client oriented metrics', you have a reason to tout this fact.

What others say and believe

As engineers, we are swayed by science, facts, and by studies and systems.

Non-engineers? Not so much.

Proof of this is simple to see. Look at all the sites on the web offering product opinions. These are not trained experts using the objective rules of science and evidence. These are people who bought or used the product or service. It's an opinion. Sometimes realistically based. Sometimes pure emotion.

As human beings, we are interested in what others think and believe. We may or may not be pushed to a conclusion, but many times we lean one way or another based on what others have experienced.

How does this apply to 'high quality'?

Buyers need to be assured they are making the correct choice. Other's

The interesting part is that this is probably true. This is what makes the myth so persistent. Your products may actually be very high quality castings!

What makes it a myth is a *belief that this makes any difference to the buyer.*

Having 'high quality' is the same as a Major League baseball owner saying he has a "high quality" team. The point here is this: In both cases, high quality, whether castings or baseball, is the *minimum* to get into the game.

Harvard Business Review[1] notes that "(metalcasters, *ed.*) stress product technology and *quality* even though *these are no longer differentiators but are simply the cost of entry.*" (author emphasis)

Why isn't science the only determinant of high quality?

People.

It's that simple.

Because people, with all their varied backgrounds, education, beliefs, and understandings.
And overuse of the phrase. Everything is now 'high quality'.

Because buyers use many different value points, there are differences in the definition, too. If buying a faucet, does a higher level of finish on the outside trump the quality of the valves and fittings? Is a gold faucet higher quality than nickel-plated?

All these make the term almost meaningless.

How to use High Quality

In order to claim 'high quality', you must have an *understandable system or standard that appeals to buyers.* When each supplier offers the same products, they are judged by buyers as 'adequate quality' for the task and the term 'high' has no meaning.

So how can you exploit the difference between your castings and the competition?

3. High Quality is viewed as a differentiator for the foundry.

> When I was an active duty Naval Officer, I helped all types of government offices buy 'off the shelf' instead of using MilSpecs. In spite of what people believe, Military Specifications or MilSpecs are only a way to ensure competition. They are not necessarily better than what commercial vendors may supply. Many times, it is the opposite. Two cases I remember clearly:
>
> > ·The MilSpec for the white undershirts men wear, was 32 pages. And few sailors bought those made to spec. They turned yellow in the ships laundry, stretched easily, and generally were lower quality. Commercially available underwear was much higher quality. In this case, MilSpec undershirts were 'lower quality' as perceived by the buyers or end users, in spite having met a 32-page requirement.
> >
> > ·The Navy bought some airliners to modify as part of an 'off-the-shelf' initiative. Then they tried to force the aircraft to fly in ways it was never built for. Flying very slowly while doing very steep turns. (You don't do that in airliners, they are designed to fly level and fast...) When the airplane didn't perform, they blamed the airplane instead of their buying effort! It was like giving a fine racing car to a farmer to plow his fields. Then when it didn't work, blaming the car instead of their buying specs and methods!
>
> In both cases, the phrase 'low quality' was used. And in both cases, it was not justified by several other factors. The T-shirts met the government's spec. Because their spec was poorly written, few bought them because of the 'quality'. The airliners had proven themselves in commercial use for years- they were high quality for the industry and designed use, but 'low quality' for this new application by the government.

The myth starts with the belief that "We have high quality castings…"

> MYTH: "Our castings are high quality".
>
> Facts: The foundry may indeed have high quality castings as measured against many different internal standards. But others in the buying cycle may have other, more subjective, 'standards'. What is 'high quality' internally to the metalcaster may not be judged the same by buyers.

The High Quality Myth

This myth frustrates!

It frustrates anyone who thinks I am calling their castings poor quality (I'm not.)
It frustrates metalcasters that buyers are not purchasing their 'high quality' castings- choosing alternate sources.

The High Quality Myth causes metalcasters to sit in frustration when buyers accept competitor's quotes. As logical engineers, it makes no sense. In fact, 'our' castings are high quality, right?

What makes this a myth?

"High quality" *becomes a myth* when any of these three beliefs are tied to it:

1. Our castings are high quality *and our competitors are not.* (Insinuated or expressed)

2. Buyers should buy OUR castings because they are high quality.

It could be a part time task for a marketing person, farmed out to a contractor, or simply done in-house by leadership.

If you kept a single client with a Client Lifetime Value of $1,000,000, the cost would pay for itself. For many years.

Want more detailed information on why customer leave? See the Loyalty Myth Addendum in the back of this book.

I can never understand...

The simplest and most effective communication is a mere 'Thank You'. Yet, I do not know of a single metalcaster who takes the time for this simple tool.

A Thank You to the client's buyer for the quote. A Thank You to the CEO of that company for the opportunity to support their needs. A Thank You to the buyer's boss, noting what a great attitude and competence the buyer showed.

Each of these builds loyalty and makes a huge impact. But it's rarely done, for reasons I can't fathom

.

*A Thank You system is almost cost free. Will you be the first to implement a **system** like this?*

- There is not enough value in the relationship

Of all the excuses for a poor relationship, this is one of the closest to screaming 'PRICE!" But it doesn't have to be. Remember, buyers have short memories. Reminding clients, regularly, of the *value* you convey to them is critical. It should be done in every communication.

Loyalty is built

Building loyalty is an integral step for any business owner who wants to have a continuous flow of revenue that is independent of price alone. (If you believe the B2B world is different, see 'My Business is Different' Myth- and reread it immediately!)

Buyers in a B2B relationship are also people.

And people are the same the world over.

They want the same things, are selfish, self-centered, and self-interested in reducing pain. Pain in their lives, especially while at work. And humans are predictable. And we are all the same, no different from them! We just don't want to think about it.

Loyalty is earned

Any metalcaster can build loyalty, but loyalty rarely grows on its own. When you plant the seeds of loyalty, it takes many steps. You do not harvest after throwing a few seeds and waiting. Like any farmer, weeding, fertilizing, and water are all key elements.

Your clients deserve the same. When you provide these, you harvest a crop of loyal clients who will do business with you over others, accept minor hiccups without screaming, and will not make a decision solely on price.

Systematizing loyalty is the best way to ensure the business is firmly planted with a good crop.

Loyalty system?

A business can create a loyalty system separately to ensure it gets the attention it deserves. It might include all of the factors listed in this section.

Why do <u>clients</u> leave?

Most metalcasters are clueless when this happens. Some believe it's price. But this is only a symptom. Just like personal relationships, it is much deeper than 'towels left on the floor in the bathroom'.

Here are some of the top reasons:

- The relationship is boring.

In our personal lives as well as business, to be boring is the ultimate sin. In metalcasting this can have several visible forms. Boring can be a lack of communication- similar to 'out of sight, out of mind', nothing new offered, or falling into a role of not appreciating your clients. Essentially, you take them for granted. Boring relationships end in divorce.

- The relationship takes too much work.

If, in the buyer's mind, it is a hassle dealing with your staff or your system, you can quickly get compared to other suppliers and come up short. Buyers pay the foundry to solve problems- not just for castings. When they spend hours calling for status updates, chasing after castings, or mistakes, or other problems, using their time to make sure the foundry is doing its job, watch out...

- You don't communicate.

Not talking about whining on the phone, calling only when there is a problem, or to advise the order will be late. This is communication about changes to the foundry that could benefit them, a buyer of the month, a new process, or other issues. Even a postcard noting 'a summer lull will allow quick turnaround on short orders' is appreciated, even if not used. Anything!

- I don't trust you anymore

Have you violated their trust? Delivered late without a decent 'heads up' and apology? Missed any deadlines, appointments, or meetings? How about your sales reps? If you use an outsider, could they be poisoning the well, unknowingly?

Any business, especially metalcasting and suppliers, can have clients.

How is this related to loyalty?

Customers are only as loyal as the next transaction or the first time they are unhappy. Then they gladly follow whoever else holds up a shiny object- which could be price, service, delivery- almost anything.

Clients, on the other hand, are under your professional care and guidance, they trust you and your service- *they rely on it*. You have tied them to you with tiny strings, so many that they are not easily broken. They want to do business with you. Refer you to others. Offer testimonials. Are willing to be Case Studies.

It's a relationship

Using a relationship analogy, customers are like girlfriends/boyfriends. Relatively easy to break up with if another comes along more to your liking. Clients are like spouses. It takes a lot to break off that binding relationship, and the results can be devastating.

Although I am not advocating *marrying* your clients, having a relationship that makes the foundry an integral and trusted cog is important. And pays off handsomely in the long run.

From diplomat school

When I was a diplomat, (hard to believe, isn't it?) one of the first points made in the school was that all countries act in their own self interests. This sounded cynical to me, but is very true. Why would a country act against its best interests? Other countries may not agree with the choices, but the leaders believe their decisions are justified as being in the best interest of the country.

This is obviously true because all countries are made up of people. And we are each selfish in all our relationships. While we try to move to other motives, it is rare indeed.

So buyers will also always act in their own self-interest. Only makes sense. That means they are not going to act in YOUR self-interest. So you had better recognize how to make your interests and theirs match.

Even if the food is good, the owners make no effort to establish a relationship, no trust building, no attempt at ensuring you always eat there. You order, you eat, you leave. And the business owner waits for another customer.

There is no *relationship* between a business and a customer. The customer is loyal for his own reasons, perhaps convenience, price, or, in this case, good food. But there are no 'ties that bind' and the next new restaurant may easily draw the customer away.

Businesses with customers do little or nothing to ensure their income next week, next month, next year, or 10 years from now.

In fact, most restaurants go broke because they have customers, not clients.

Many other businesses, including foundries, suffer the same fate.

Clients

A client, on the other hand, is someone who comes under your care and professional guidance. You become the trusted advisor. You have the answers, have built up the trust, and communicate regularly. Clients enter a system that establishes a long term relationship.

Lawyers and accountants have clients. (Other than that, I am no fan of lawyers…)

Unless the lawyer or accountant screws up by violating trust, communication, or moral limits, clients remains with them for a lifetime- and possibly beyond. Loyalty is an essential part of the relationship. As is trust. So a lawyer builds up a 'practice'- a loyal group of clients that are all but guaranteed to provide his income in the future.

The equivalent in the medical community used to be a patient.

Sadly, because the medical community seems to be falling off the wagon, their patients are becoming 'customers.' In the past however, a doctor had a 'cradle to grave' relationship with his or her patients (clients). He was there at the birth and took care of his patient for their lifetime or until he retired. That doctor was assured an income because his patients wouldn't consider going anywhere else.

times of trouble.

Customers versus Clients

I routinely used the word 'client' throughout this book. Although you may believe that 'client' and 'customer' are interchangeable, I do not. And the difference is very significant.

> ### Some Clients are Ds
>
> One of my coaches, Dan Kennedy, told me a story. Remember cassettes? Years ago he had a cassette duplicating service. It was for speakers who sold training programs. He had a client phone him in a dead panic because his cassettes had been lost in transit to the speaking engagement. The speaker sold thousands of dollars at these engagements. He would lose a lot of sales if the tapes did not arrive. Dan went into overtime reproducing more, shipping them express overnight. His quick actions saved the event for the speaker who sold over $15K of products, a sizable chunk in the 1970's.
>
> It wasn't three months later that the client took his business somewhere else. Why? For a lower price. How much lower? A SINGLE PENNY per cassette. Dan's 'save the day' efforts were forgotten.
>
> The client's loyalty was zero.
>
> You have dealt with people like this in your business. They are C and D clients. (D's should be sent elsewhere, they aren't worth the effort, tarnish your reputation, and make an excellent referral for someone you don't like.)

Customers

Customers make a purchase. That's it.

Consider the local family owned restaurant.

The Loyalty Myth

Myth: "My customers are loyal, they won't take their business elsewhere."

Fact: Customers are only as loyal as you make them. Make no effort, they will chase lowest price, better customer service, higher trust, less hassles. And the only ones who will remain are those no one

"In business, staying with a vendor who doesn't appreciate you isn't loyalty, it's stupidity. Why work with someone who doesn't appreciate your business?"

Many business owners, not just in the metalcasting field, believe their customers are loyal.
Nothing could be further from the truth.

Just like the simple statement opening this chapter, loyalty is a function of several factors. Ok, unless you have a dog. They are probably loyal no matter how poorly they are treated.

People are different

And that simple phrase captures the heart and soul of why people are not loyal to businesses. Especially in the B2B world. Buyers are not appreciated enough to treat them any differently.

The Loyalty Myth is simply a belief that 'our customers are loyal' with no attention, appreciation, additional communication, or effort. Following the myth leads to shock when customers leave, or more appropriately, *flee* in

Notes

[1] New York Times, "Behind Gold's Glitter: Torn Lands and Pointed Questions" June 14, 2010

year are closing in the United States alone.

Are you hiding in a comfortable place, hunkered down, afraid?

Are you OPEN to new ideas and concepts? The great industrialist Henry Ford had the best summary of this concept: "If you always do what you've always done, you'll always get what you've always got."

Raise Your Right Hand

And swear: "I will consider new opportunities, I will find what works with other industries. I will research why other metalcasters and suppliers are making good profits. I will have an open mind."
You can break MBID.

Ask me how to display your new confidence when you see me at a presentation…

Was I right?

I told you at the beginning this would be an ugly topic.

Was this harsh?

Business is harsh.

I am not looking to make friends.

I want metalcasters to make money. And some are unsuited to the task.

If MBID still keeps a warm place in your heart, don't contact me. PLEASE!

All successful businesses are led by researchers.

In a foundry, reducing the scrap rate, otherwise known as defect analysis and correction, is vital. Testing different methods is critical to this effort.

To solve revenue defects and reduce the 'scrap rate', researchers are constantly testing better ways to satisfy clients, engender more loyalty, differentiate their foundry, and become trusted advisors.

Researching how to differentiate their foundry to attract more 'A' clients. And, like any researcher, this includes constant testing. Nothing good was ever discovered except through hard work and testing.

It's all about attitude

Are you constantly learning?

> *Don't think positioning and differentiation is important?*
>
> *Everyone has heard of Pike's Peak in Colorado. But it isn't the tallest. There are 19 other peaks above it.*
>
> *Can you name a single one? Bet you can't...*
>
> *You can develop the same differentiation for your metalcasting or supplier business...*

One way to overcome MBID is with learning. And learning about ALL phases of the metalcasting BUSINESS, not just melting metal. There are large groups of people that can help with the technical expertise.

Very few with the revenue defect analysis.

Follow the crowd?

Are you doing what everyone else does? I offer this simple truism: if you do what the average competitor does, you're guaranteed, at best, average results. Most of your competitors are struggling. That's why 50 foundries a

3% success rate, it would be abandoned by most foundries. Unless the profit from the successful 3% made the investment worthwhile. (Hardly likely.)

But in the area of revenue, a 3% success rate with current and potential clients can generate millions of dollars in new business. Yes, 97% of the money spent was wasted, but the ROI (Return-on-Investment) can easily be 30:1. Incredible but true.

The scrap rate is too high

There is always waste. Efforts to get new clients/quotes, get existing clients to spend more, or to ask for quotes more often, are no different.

Phineas T Barnum (PT Barnum) was famous for his ability to bring in people to his business. But he was even quoted as saying: "Half of all my money spent on marketing is wasted. If only I could figure out which half!"

The gold industry turns 30 tons of dirt to find an ounce of gold[1]. That is a scrap rate of 99.99999%! So how could they stay in business? Very simply, this is a flawed measurement.

For the average believer in MBID, the 'scrap rate' for investments in new quotes/revenue/buyers is viewed incorrectly. Instead of looking at the investment using such nebulous numbers as 'response rate', leads, or 'Likes', use Client Lifetime Value (CLV) and ROI.

Client Lifetime Value and ROI

Flawed thinking and logic says "I spent $15,000 and only got one new customer".

CLV/ROI says "I spent $15,000 and got one new customer who will probably spend $150,000 during his time as our customer."

That is the realistic way of looking at an investment. Client Lifetime Value, discussed in the accompanying Numbers book, shows a 10-to-1 payback for the money invested. That's an ROI you will rarely find with investments in new machinery.

Are you constantly testing?

And the easiest to overcome if you have an open mind.

Many metalcasters try a new idea or concept to fix revenue defects, and it 'doesn't work'. But, like many of the myths in this book, it is usually a false conclusion.

Like the person trying to lose weight, who diets for two days and then quits in frustration. 'Dieting doesn't work' they conclude.

Or the person who doesn't run, but wants to win a marathon. After 3 days of running, they give up. Can't be done, they mistakenly conclude.

The town barber had seen growth all around him. His business had also grown.

One day, the building across the street started undergoing renovation. Soon a new 'Men's Hair Salon' opened, boasting 'All Haircuts $5'.

He was stunned. $5? And the salon was huge!

How could he compete? He couldn't lower his price and survive.

In desperation, he called in a consultant.

Two days later, everyone sitting in the salon looked out the window and saw the new sign across the street, which loudly proclaimed:

It ain't easy

There are no 'easy buttons' in this business. Even less when it comes to fixing revenue and sales defects. At least there are plenty of rules, formulas and algorithms that can be invoked in an effort to correct casting defects. And the 'simplicity' of dealing with casting defects can obscure the 'fuzzier' methods of revenue defect correction.

Revenue Defects are Different

Look at it this way. If a casting effort had a 97% scrap rate, meaning only

YOU control who you hang out with. If you find that everyone agrees with your 'victim' point of view, you need new friends, colleagues, staff, assistants.

YOU control the business, not anyone else. Unless you allow them to take control. Others in the industry have control. Study them. Meet them. Understand them.

YOU can learn from the mistakes of others. While learning what worked for others, find out what didn't.

YOU can learn from other industries. Metalcasting is a business niche, not a standalone, far away, galaxy. Know where Ray Croc of McDonalds® fame, came up with the drive-in concept? He saw it at a bank. Where would that company be today if he had said "My Business is Different".

Feeling of Helplessness

The feeling of helplessness affects all entrepreneurs and business leaders at one time or another. It's not unusual. The maddening situations that continually appear make successful metalcasters experts at playing "Whack-a-Mole" when they take the kids and grandkids to the arcade.

But the feelings should be dispersed with rest and relaxation to bring a recharge. Or they must be dealt with. Hunkering down into MBID can be suicidal to the business, hopefully not the individual. The 'overwhelmness' is normal. Succumbing to it is not.

I do not present myself as an expert in psychiatry or psychology. But a tenacious hold onto MBID may need professional intervention.

down into MBID can be suicidal to the business, hopefully not the individual. The 'overwhelm-ness' is normal. Succumbing to it is not.

I do not present myself as an expert in psychiatry or psychology. But a tenacious hold onto MBID may need professional intervention.

I tried it, it didn't work

Of all the reasons for MBID, this one may be the most understandable.

will annoy you.
As a minimum.
Enrage you, possibly.

Only you can change

If you are easily insulted by a close examination of the truth, either get your adult pants on and continue reading, or put the book down now. I cannot talk you out of MBID, it's a choice each person makes. But the facts can be presented.

You've been burned

From my experience across consumer, industrial, government, and military sectors, MBID is actually a response to one of these issues:
- Loss of Control/ I am a victim of circumstances
- Feelings of Helplessness
- Lack of Success/ I tried "it" and it didn't work.

This is not psychology

I am not a shrink and this is not a substitute for professional help. (The lawyers should be happy with that disclaimer…)

Loss of Control

Most of us are 'Type A' personalities who value control. When things beyond our control buffet us, we get unnerved. The economy, government, buyers, staff, workforce, competitors- the list is endless if you want to blame others for your predicament.

Compare it to driving down the interstate when suddenly a piece of scrap falls from the bed of the truck in front of you. Do you simply drive over it blaming the trucker? Or do you swerve quickly, hoping to miss it, but ready in case you do hit it?

There will always be some factors out of your control. So the real answer is to take control of those things you can instead of sitting back.

YOU control who is your client. If you don't like your clients, get new ones!

My Business is Different Myth

"A mind is like a parachute. It doesn't work if it is not open." *Frank Zappa*

"If someone is able to show me that what I think or do is not right, I will happily change, for I seek the truth, by which no one was ever truly harmed. It is the person who continues in his self-deception and ignorance who is harmed." *Marcus Aurelius*

> Myth: "My Business is different. None of this will work. I've tried it all. There is nothing I can do. I am a ping-pong ball on the ocean. Woe is me."
>
> Fact: If making money in metalcasting was easy, everyone would do it. You can blame everyone else, refuse to try anything new. Or realize other foundry leadership teams are thriving and growing under the same circumstances. Same economic challenges, overseas competitors, government regulation, lousy buyers. Hmmm.

Why is this first?

Not everyone believes this myth, but it is the single strongest myth in metalcasting. If this applies to you, this will not be a fun read. But it may offer you the hope of change from at least knowing why you feel this way.

Warning

I will warn readers right now. If you believe your business is different from every other one in the world, and therefore no solutions work, this chapter

THE MYTHS

The author can be reached through Debby@TheFoundryMarketer.com with your questions or to arrange a private consultation.

These are the same people who stay in their homes during floods, hurricanes, and tornadoes. Ignoring the obvious, believing it won't affect them. These are the ones who evolution describes as 'soon to be eliminated from the gene pool'. They don't care as long as there is no friction, no fence bending, no thought required.

And there are those who will defend the dragons. They not only won't help you eliminate the myths, they may actually work against the effort.

These people are the most dangerous.

They have such a strong belief in the myth that they will mount up in their defense. Challenge you personally, your role as a leader, and question your abilities. Like a lion guarding her young, they will tear at every bone and sinew they can get to keep their beliefs alive and intact. While you are throwing a life ring, they are screaming "Swim faster! Ignore the sharks! The water is fine! There are no waves" as the poor person slips below into the blue darkness.

When you finally overcome the myths, you then implement the metrics.

Sadly, this methodology, conquering myths first, may also be like chasing butterflies- exhausting and rarely fruitful.

The second way

The second way, and the one I advocate as the most efficient, is to implement the metrics first.

You will still get those who don't believe in their usefulness, who prefer doing what they've always done. Some will take the metrics as 'gobbledygook' with no possibility of being useful. They will cite chapter and verse from some old college text to prove they were never taught these numbers. Others will question.

But implementation and repeated use of the numbers wins over the doubters, taking the fire out of the fire breathing dragons. When your management team sees the results for themselves, it is easier to eliminate the myths that have tied you down the way an anchor holds a ship.

Whichever you choose, there is help available if you are confused or feel overwhelmed.

And vice versa.

The myths will turn your business upside down, too, if you follow them. But the metrics, once applied in a system, will turn all the myths on their head. It becomes so obvious that they are myths, blasting them out of the business no longer needs dynamite- a simple pry bar will work.

So it isn't just a funny way to print a book, there is a real reason for the method. As you read one book or the other, keep in mind that these are two sides of the same coin.

Remember:

Avoid the MYTHS

Follow the METRICS

Two Ways To Success

There are two ways to success using this two-in-one book. You have a choice. One is not necessarily better than the other, although I do personally have a preference. Each organizational leadership team will need to evaluate the best tool for change in the environment they have.

The first way

You can go after the myths first and slay them as a gallant knight slays dragons.

And in keeping with that picture, the journey will be full of challenges. Some will argue with these points and claim they are not myths. People argued the earth was flat. The Flat Earth Society is still active. So don't be discouraged by their 'facts won't convince me' mentality.

Others will claim there is nothing that can be done- there are always dragons so live with it. This group has no interest in change, no matter how much evidence their lifestyle, fortune, and business are all under threat. The status quo gives them comfort. They don't have to learn anything new.

But for those who want to make progress, want to win more quotes, bring more stability to their business, and build a lifestyle and reputation unmatched, this is the place to start.

Expect overlap

You will see extensive overlap in some of the areas. Why? Because a solution to one myth can affect others. When you read that communication can solve the Loyalty Myth, keep in mind it may also be part of the solution to the Quote System Myth.

Know why cannibals don't eat clowns?
Because they taste funny...

Why is this book 'backwards?

Reading the myths book *feels* funny.

That's deliberate.

The difference between the myths that you must overcome and the metrics that will propel your foundry to success are so different, yet so related, I struggled with a way to show this. I finally settled on making two distinct books but published so that you had to make a real effort to change topics.

And believing the myths is exactly backwards from using the numbers.

builds up inside us until it's healthily released, dates back to the Greeks, was revived by Freud, and gained steam during the "let it all hang out" 1960s of punching bags and primal screams. But the catharsis hypothesis is a myth- a plausible one, and elegant one, but a myth nonetheless. Scores of studies have shown that venting doesn't soothe anger; it fuels it." (Source: *Quiet* by Susan Cain pg 233)

The Desert Trip
Or how about the 'ration your water in the desert' myth. Sadly, people can actually die if they follow this one. Your body needs water much more than food. And it must be hydrated or the brain starts to lose capability (dry out??), and the body becomes useless. While you wait until tomorrow to drink your water ration, your body shuts down. (You will see a form of this myth when you read about cutting costs to increase profits in the Source of Profit Myth.)

Root of all evil
Most myths are misinterpretations of what is observed. Or what is said.

Have you heard "Money is the root of all evil"? Almost everyone has. And then inwardly questioned how in the world we would ever get along without money? This quote is a myth.

The real quote is "The LOVE of money is the root of all evil". Don't believe me? Many don't. But check out any bible. Timothy's first letter, chapter 6, verse 10.

One of Two

This book is one of two that outlines the result of an intense review of the actions of metalcasters who eventually closed. This book deals with the myths that were evident. The other book examines numbers that could have been used to focus on solutions before the bankruptcies.

Controversial

Are these points controversial? Of course. No one likes to change their way of thinking. And these are very much 'in your face'. No holds barred. It is designed to allow introspection by those who truly want to change.

If you bought this book hoping to prove these are not true in the industry, you wasted money. Your attitude will stop you from learning.

Introduction to the Myths

"Long-term commitment to new learning and new philosophy is required of any management that seeks transformation. The timid and the fainthearted, and the people that expect quick results, are doomed to disappointment." William Edwards Deming

The purpose of this book is to identify the myths that appeared to close foundries.

However, I cannot just name these myths. That would do little for those who want to eliminate them. So each of the myths has other commentary dealing with identifying examples, proving their falsity (nice word, huh?) or helping the reader to expunge them from the organization.

Myths everywhere

Myths are not isolated to any one field.

There is a persistent myth based on 'crystal skulls' supposedly found in South America. Indiana Jones fans will immediately recognize what I am referring to. The myth is especially persistent because of three actual crystal skulls which were displayed in the British Museum of Natural History, a museum in Paris, and one sent to the Smithsonian Institute.

The skulls were on display in Paris and London for over 50 years before being proven to be *complete frauds*. Scientific investigation showed modern tools were used to create the skulls.

But the myth persists to this day.

Scream if you like

Another myth is the 'catharsis hypothesis'. This myth, *" that aggression*

the metrics is a subtler way to crush the myths, because instead of arguing with your staff, you simply use the numbers to find and analyze defects- a system- instead of the voodoo of blaming the myths.

Get reading- and implementing!

[1]http://online.wsj.com/news/articles/SB10001424052702304851104579361451951384512

book is not an indicator of importance.

This is because every foundry or supplier believing in one or more myths will have a completely different combination, and in differing proportions.

Read them all, analyze the situation in your company, and consider the ways to change.

Parallel reading

The Numbers book can be read in parallel. The numbers offer solutions to help overcome the myths. The books are actually paired, but can be read separately or only singly.

As I note whenever I give a presentation on the myths and metrics, there are two ways to overcome:

Eliminate the Myths, then employ the metrics

This approach may be more difficult but it can be done.

To eliminate the myths will require taking on dragons.

You must convince others in the organization the myths are not true, they have no basis in reality, and that others have already been down this road.

You must challenge long held beliefs. And be tenacious in redirecting the energy away from the easy answer- myths.

Only the strongest will survive this approach. CEOs can do it, VPs of Marketing will have to answer the long line of doubters who parade into the CEO/President/Owners office to sway against your campaign.
It may take years to prove your case.

For a simpler approach, consider the alternative discussed next.

Use the Metrics to eliminate the myths

This is the more successful approach.

By employing the number/metrics, and using them to analyze the defects, the myths are eventually either exploded or expunged over time. And using

OTHER NOTES

Each myth can be read separately

You can jump around- pick and choose- what you want to read. I do recommend reading and understanding them all. But the order is not nearly as important as overcoming the myth with the information you learn.

One other warning: Reading and overcoming a few myths is like squishing just a few ants at a picnic. It won't get the solutions you want unless you eliminate them all!

Each myth stands alone although they also interact

Each of the myths is a single problem. Each stands on its own legs, wreaking havoc throughout a metalcaster's business. But there is also interaction as one myth feeds belief in another, is fed from others, and can be justified by one another. You will learn the most when you read and understand each one, then consider closely the interactions within your own business model.

As an example, the Quality Myth is a ghost worth exorcising (not exERcising…). But the Quality myth reinforces several of the other myths, including the My Business is Different myth. In this case, 'my business is different because we have high quality' is typical thinking. Another example: believing in the 'Buyers Only Buy on Price' myth provides the reasoning for the 'Source of Profit' myth. Thus, the belief that lowering costs is the only way to increase profits.

Eliminating one myth does not eliminate the effect of others.

They are not arranged in any order

Although one may be more predominant than the others, their order in this

any degree is only a 'license to learn'. What works so perfectly in the hallowed halls of the ivory tower probably doesn't have the same simplicity in the real world.

by the "Buyers Only Buy on Price" misperception.

Why haven't I heard this before?

To my knowledge, no one has taken the risk to expose these myths.

Some metalcasters will argue the points, a few will get red in the face in denial. Some will loudly return to their old ways and blame competition, the economy, labor cost- everything but themselves.

So be it. I can't help everyone.

Few embraced Galileo when he taught the earth revolved around the sun. The Flat Earth Society is still active- just look it up on the web! (theflatearthsociety.org) And some people in the industry are still thinking in medieval terms.

But I am committed to growth and profits to those who are willing to take up the truth and march forward, instead of shrinking back in fear of every dark night. This small group will become the core of growth in the future, leveraging their expertise, and overcoming every obstacle. They will become great places to work, because every day will be in the bright light of profitability.

Some of these myths were taught as facts in school. How could that be?

There are many myths throughout the world. Some even get full academic recognition!

My most recent example is zombies. These totally mythical 'creatures' are gaining ground on college campuses according to an article in 2014's Wall Street Journal[1]. The article notes colleges that 'teach' courses on zombies. And 'scholarly books' have been written.

Sorry to burst anyone's bubble, but zombies are a complete myth.

Remember that history is filled with 'facts' that are eventually shown to be either false or poorly formed rationale. The earth used to be the center of the universe, bathing was considered dangerous, life sprang from stagnant water, and alchemists could turn lead into gold.
While many business ideas are taught in school, the smart graduates know

Charles Blondin, the tightrope walker, had strung a cable across Niagara Falls.

He repeatedly dazzled the crowds with his exploits that included, among other feats, walking blindfolded, and carrying a chair on which he sat midway across the falls.

On this day, he had traversed back and forth and asked the crowd:

"Do you believe I can push a wheelbarrow across and back?"

"We believe, we believe" they shouted, almost in unison.

After successfully completing his transit, he asked the crowd if they believed he could do it again, this time pushing the wheelbarrow.

"We believe, we believe!!" came the loud chorus.

Again he went over and returned safely. He then asked if the crowd believed he could go across and back with a person in the wheelbarrow.

"We believe, we believe!!" the now frenzied masses responded.

"So who will ride in the wheelbarrow?" the tightrope walker asked.

There was a deathly silence.

Which myth is the most common?

That is a challenging question. The most predominant, even from active metalcasters, is the "My Business is Different" myth followed very closely

Statistics and metrics, more scientific data, can be used to justify a reader's inaction. If, for example, statistics showed each of the foundries had advertised in a specific format, readers could mistakenly alleviate concern for their own business by smugly affirming "We don't do that..."

False conclusion.

So the myths speak for themselves in general terms.

Did every closed foundry believe in every myth?

Believe is too strong a phrase as it suggests they were aware of their actions.

Every one demonstrated a belief, even if they didn't recognize it. In most cases, I refer to this as 'accidental ignorance'. Most were not aware of the points in this book. It's not that they aggressively denied them. They just never heard of them. It wasn't a deliberate attempt to fly in the face of the facts presented here.

It wasn't head in the sand thinking (horrible analogy for the metalcasting industry!). It was more like an accident. So I use the term accidental ignorance.

For example, if you don't wear a seatbelt, you have *demonstrated* a belief that you will never get in an automobile accident. You may not actually make that declaration but the actions point to the belief.

Without getting into semantics on a large scale, the word believe means 'to understand a point to where it changes your actions'.

This true story makes the point.

No one who was willing to take action, thus their 'belief' was mere words

If you, too, fail to take action, your belief in your foundry, employees, and profits has no basis.

Questions I get about this book

Who should read this book?

Any CEO who is ready to face the truth, but wants to know where the dragons really lay.

Any President on a quest for excellence in revenue and sales, not just castings.

Any owner who wants to ferret out those ideas and beliefs that are holding back the business.

Any owner who has recognized the truth of "If you always do what you've always done, you'll always get what you've always got." But still needs to identify why it's true at his plant.

Any marketing person who struggles with those who don't get it, those who want formulas, who would rather believe myths than reality.

Each will find surprising answers here.

How did you discover the myths?

Twenty-three closed foundries were the initial focus. Each myth was discovered based on observation of actions, media interviews, actual accounting details when available, websites, and historical information covering many areas. The myths have been constantly revised as more data from more metalcasters become available.

Was this a scientific study?

No, not by a long shot...

Does that invalidate the conclusions?

No, not by a long shot…

Who is Mark Mehling?

Mark has a rich background across several areas. He is the only Metalcaster/Supplier Management Advisor dedicated to fixing defects in revenue. His P2/DARE system implements a web based dashboard for metalcast leaders to instantly know the key indicators of a foundry's health, numbers no accountant ever tracks.

He is the ongoing author of the *Shaping Strategy* column, published in the American Foundry Society's **MODERN CASTING** magazine. Mark has presented in the most recent American Foundry Society (AFS) Metalcasting Congress in the US and to a standing-room only crowd at the World Foundry Congress. He publishes the monthly **M4 SHORT SHEET** (see bonuses) and the paid subscription "**UGLY Marketing Newsletter for Metalcasters and Suppliers**".

Mark was selected as the "Service Marketer of the Year" by GKIC, a 25,000+ association of marketing professionals, and is a certified copywriter. He has been a Naval Aviator, a Diplomat, and flies a private business jet. He and his bride live in Florida with three parrots (yes, he's nuts!).

What's In This Book

- ❖ *Who is Mark Mehling*
- ❖ *Questions I get about the book*
- ❖ *Other Notes*
- ❖ *Introduction to the Myths*
- ❖ *Why is this Book Read Backwards?*
- ❖ *My Business is Different*
- ❖ *The Loyalty Myth*
- ❖ *The High Quality Myth*
- ❖ *The Source of Profit Myth*
- ❖ *The Quote System Myth*
- ❖ *Buyers Only Buy on Price Myth*
- ❖ *The Source of Revenue Myth*
- ❖ *Other Foundry Myths*
- ❖ *Addendums*
- ❖ *Congratulations*
- ❖ *BONUSES*

7 Myths That Shackle Foundry Profit$
(and suppliers, too!)

Which do you believe?
Which ones are stealing money
in your metal casting business?

Mark Mehling

www.ingramcontent.com/pod-product-compliance
Lightning Source LLC
Chambersburg PA
CBHW060548200326
41521CB00007B/527